# GOD
## Money
## & ME

**PUBLISHED BY:**

LIFE RESOURCE INTERNATIONAL

Eden Business Park, Level 3, Eden 4

14 Normanby Road, Mt Eden, Auckland 1024

New Zealand

P: +64 9 306 4222

F: +64 9 306 4223

Email: gmm@lifenz.org

**COVER AND TEXT DESIGNED BY:**

Katie Wilson

**PRINTED IN AUSTRALIA BY:**

Griffin Press

168 Cross Keys Rd

Salisbury South

South Australia 5106

ISBN: 978-0-473-39685-5

A catalog record for this book is available from the National Library of New Zealand.

# ENDORSEMENTS

"Paul de Jong's book and four-week curriculum, *God Money &
Me*, is the outcome of many years committed to finding a pathway
to financial breakthrough based on biblical principles. His honest
style and insight will give you renewed hope and the understanding
needed to see God's promised blessings."
**Robert Morris**
Founding Senior Pastor, *Gateway Church, Dallas/Fort Worth, Texas*
Bestselling Author of *The Blessed Life, The God I Never Knew, Truly
Free,* and *Frequency*

"Undoubtedly one of my most longstanding friends and loyal
confidantes, Pastor Paul de Jong is a leader with a generous heart.
Over many years I have watched him live what he preaches and
I believe that you will be impacted by his wisdom and pastoral
insights into living a generous, accountable, and fruitful life that
overflows with the blessings of God."
**Brian Houston**
Global Senior Pastor, *Hillsong Church*

"*God Money & Me* tackles one of the trickiest issues so many of us face: the intersection of our faith and our finances. With his typical unique insights and firsthand experiences, Paul de Jong unlocks the *Bible's* perspective on money and reveals a practical pathway that all of us can follow. Paul shows us how to live as responsible stewards of what God has entrusted to us as we also experience the financial freedom that comes from faithful obedience. I just know God will use this book to inform, encourage and liberate so many people about the power of money in their lives."
**Chris Hodges**
Senior Pastor, *Church of the Highlands*
Author of *Fresh Air* and *The Daniel Dilemma*

"Pastor Paul de Jong presents a personal and hard-won under-standing of the role money plays in our lives in this passionate examination of scriptural teaching on material wealth. If you feel you're fighting a losing battle with your bank balance, you'll find empowering answers for money management that will bless you spiritually as well as financially."
**Tommy Barnett**
Pastor, *Dream City Church, Phoenix & Los Angeles Dream Center, Los Angeles*

"Pastor Paul de Jong's new book, *God Money & Me*, is an empow-ering message of financial freedom and blessing. You will receive wisdom and revelation on the practical issues of financial success as well as the spiritual issues that make a difference. Paul's life is a story of success in ministry and business, and financial realms. His personal insights and biblical perspectives will encourage you to new levels of victory over greed, debt and pressure. Dive into *God Money & Me* today – you will be blessed."
**Casey Treat**
Senior Pastor, *Christian Faith Center*

"What an amazing book this is! Paul brings his unique and refreshing insights in this extremely valuable book providing teaching on one of the most needed subjects for Christians everywhere. This will be such a blessing to leaders, churches and people in all walks and professions. Thanks for writing this, Paul. Love it."
**Phil Pringle**
Founder and President, *C3 Church International*

"Pastor Paul de Jong's *Bible* based take on the topic of God and money is something this generation desperately needs. *God Money & Me* is a relevant, straight to the point guide on God's plan for our finances."
**Jentezen Franklin**
Senior Pastor, *Free Chapel*
*New York Times* Best-Selling Author

"The ability to steward financial seed affects every aspect of our lives. Too often we neglect the necessary conversation this book addresses in *God Money & Me*. Pastor Paul applies years of wisdom and brings practical insight to help lift and shift perspectives from living in financial fear to discovering financial freedom."
**Charlotte Gambill**
Lead Pastor, *LIFE Church, UK*
Author of *The Miracle In the Middle*

"Money is at the center of our daily lives but not many know how to handle it well. Everyone wants it but not everyone is comfortable to talk about it openly. I want to thank my friend, Paul de Jong, for his courage in pouring into this book some of his wisdom and experience in handling money as he walks with God. I believe this book will greatly bless you."
**Jeffrey Rachmat**
Senior Pastor, *Jakarta Praise Community Church*

"*God Money & Me*, like everything Pastor Paul de Jong teaches, comes from the transparent heart of a leader whose greatest desire is to see God's people free to walk in authority and power. When it comes to finances, people have a wide range of perspectives on how money is made, how it should be used, and why it matters. Pastor Paul bases every section of this important book on God's word, and guides us through his own (sometimes painful) experience to a place of revelation and ultimately, the breakthrough we all seek. *God Money & Me* is one of the simplest and clearest illustrations of how to be fruitful, generous, and build a life of financial freedom that resources the kingdom and enables you to leave an inheritance for your 'children's children.'"

**Steve Kelly**
Senior Pastor, *WAVE Church, USA*

# CONTENTS

# FOREWORD

As I write this foreword I am sitting in a hotel on the African continent. Undeniably, the fifty-four countries that together comprise the African continent make it the richest geographical mass – past, present and into the foreseeable future.

However, the irony is not lost on the world that many humanitarian relief efforts are focused on the African continent as well.

While many wiser than me have opinions on this most blatant disparity, I also think that the same happens in the lives of individuals – worldwide. So many available resources, yet such blatant lack.

In *God Money & Me* and its accompanying curriculum, my friend Pastor Paul de Jong has created a resource that will free and empower the reader financially into generosity. The thirty one succinct chapters are full of insight, wisdom and practical applicability.

I love the blend of inspiration and instruction, leading to

understanding and living the life you were meant to live.

Mention the word 'money' and the response ranges from hesitance to fear tinged with experienced cynicism. Not so with this book.

You will read it. You will encourage your family and friends to read it. You will have your small groups study it, and grow and become financially free and even more generous as a result. Your generosity will spill into your church and other kingdom ventures. All this will happen when you embark on the path to financial freedom.

I've known Pastor Paul for many years – publicly and privately. This book personifies him. The messenger is the message.

**Sam Chand**
Leadership Consultant
Author of *Bigger Faster Leadership*

# ACKNOWLEDGEMENTS

First and foremost, I want to thank Jesus, for giving me a life that is abundant and beyond measure in every way. Thank you, Holy Spirit, for hearing my cry for help and leading me to the pathway of financial freedom. Your grace, faithfulness, wisdom and strength has enabled me to continue to learn and grow.

To my wife Maree, you are and have always been my best friend. It has been your unending support that has empowered me to live a life that reaches into the second mile. My incredible children and grandchildren, I love each one of you more than words could ever express.

To Jenny, Jonno and Liz, your willingness, wisdom and hard work have enabled me to see this dream in my heart become a living reality. Also to all those who over many years have continued to believe in me and encouraged me to put pen to paper in regards to bringing hope in this major area of financial freedom, thank you. To you, the reader of *God Money & Me*, thank you also for taking the time to pursue greater clarity in the area of your finances, which will have a profound impact on the generations that come after you. Finally, thank you to my amazing LIFE family, who are the community we get to do life with. Your continued love and support has encouraged me to keep reaching beyond what I had believed to be my limitations.

# INTRODUCTION

---

Have you ever felt trapped, living with a growing sense that when it comes to money you've got no way out? Like many others, this was my financial world. I thought I was living generously and honoring God, but I was not experiencing His promised blessing.

To explain a little better, let's turn back the clock. Years ago, as a young New Zealand pastor and family man, I was in America shopping at one of those super huge hardware stores, when I saw a lawn mower on sale at less than half the price they were at home. Even better, this machine had an engagement handle that drove the wheels and made mowing practically automatic! I had never seen a mower like it – in fact, I wasn't aware they even existed. Not only that, but it had a key electric start while those at home were limited to pull start.

Months later, courtesy of a good friend, my fancy new mower was finally delivered. Excitedly I opened the box and simply couldn't wait to get it going. I put in oil and fuel, bent down to start it – and nothing happened. No motor, no engine noise, no vibrations.

I couldn't work it out. Why didn't the key start it? Was the battery charged? Or had I bought a lemon? I noticed there was a pull handle to start the engine manually. So I pulled it – and the motor roared into life. Breakthrough!

So I cut my lawns, and the new mower was amazing – but I was still ticked off that the key electric start didn't work. Next time I brought it out, I tried the key again, and again, no response. I reluctantly accepted it didn't work as promised and used it with limited functioning. Then about a year later, for some reason, I pulled the wheel engagement handle and tried the key at the same time. Instant success! Couldn't believe my ears! After a year of the electric start not working, it roared into life. That's when I had to accept I was the typical male. I'd never read the instruction manual. For the key to work, you had to pull the wheel engagement handle into position. The key start was never faulty; I just hadn't taken the time to learn how to work it properly.

That mower is a perfect analogy for why so many of us feel trapped by money. We operate our finances like I was using that mower, going about it, unaware of important information contained in the user's manual. If we read and follow the manual, God promises to personally lead us into financial freedom. God has laid out clear answers for us, showing how we can operate in a dimension that will empower our lives in ways 'immeasurably more than all we ask or imagine' (*Ephesians 3:20,* NIV). But the 'guidelines for God's economy' may differ widely from your expectations. And they are only effective once you understand how to 'turn the key' while engaging His principles.

In *God Money & Me,* you'll find vital information affecting your natural, financial and spiritual life. Without even knowing it, many of us live under the domination of money. All too often we don't stop long enough to discover God's full and complete plan so we fail to walk the pathway that leads to financial release. Every one of us, according to the *Bible*, can discover godly wisdom on how to manage money and experience breakthrough into a positive financial future.

I believe this book will bring you a biblical perspective on prosperity. We will discover that biblical prosperity is a God-ordained concept. In this context, prosperity is no longer a 'bad word'. It's a 'God word' and a 'good word'. God is a big God, a prosperous and abundant God. He wants to smash our limited thinking about money – the stunted ideas that have held many of God's children back. Scripture gives us the complete solution for a sound financial future. Sustainable change comes about not through wishful thinking, but from understanding and applying scripture to our circumstances.

In *God Money & Me* we will learn how to build a foundation for financial freedom by discovering:
- Why money has a hold on us
- A biblical perspective on prosperity
- God-centered wisdom on money
- How to break the power of debt
- How to build a financial future

Money – or the lack of it – influences more of our decisions about our lives than any other single factor. I encourage you to not start at the end but to read part by part, and to work through the study guide as you go. Let's get started.

# PART ONE
# MONEY MYTHS

# ONE

# WHAT THE DEVIL KNOWS THAT BELIEVERS DON'T

---

Have you ever found yourself in a disagreement with someone close to you over the subject of money? It could be that someone wants to spend, and you want to save. Or friends want to dine out in cafes and restaurants, while you would rather conserve money and cook at home.

Did you know that nearly 50 percent of couples who get divorced do so because of disagreements and contention over money? And, in addition to that, for approximately 70 percent of newlyweds, money is the issue that causes most of the arguments in their first year.

Whoever we are, money has a far greater authority over our lives than we have ever considered. In *God Money & Me*, I hope to show you how you can experience freedom from the power money exercises over your daily decisions. Because for the majority of us, it determines where we live, where we work, our level of debt, and practically all our life-shaping decisions.

You may disagree. You may tell yourself that 'money doesn't own me'. Really? How many times have you promised yourself you will do something significant with your life, then paused and then declared, '… once I have paid off that loan, put some extra savings aside, got a better-paying job, when I finally have control of my finances'?

And how often have you felt yourself react when asked for money? 'Oh, not again – do they think I'm made of money?' Even though it may be a request for a donation for a worthy cause, we seem to have so many other priorities making a demand on the money we currently possess.

## WHAT'S IN IT FOR ME?

Right from the outset, I want to communicate clearly in *God Money & Me* that we can be freed from the shackles of our life decisions becoming dictated by money. There is no doubt God has a plan, clearly outlined in the *Bible*, for financial freedom. I believe one of our greatest hindrances is that this subject hasn't been taught holistically, and therefore when it comes to money, we live with no clear game plan or financial pathway. Dare I say it, money has become such a fiercely debated topic in Christianity partly because we don't really understand the authority money has and we have had little focused teaching. I believe the enemy knows that if we live with a true biblical revelation in regard to money, we all would unlock a newfound liberty both personally and for God's kingdom.

It is interesting that research indicates that one important reason people leave the Church is they feel it is more interested in getting their money than in them personally. Years of studies carried out by the Francis A. Schaeffer Institute of Church Leadership Development have validated these findings.

There is no doubt the subject of money is a hot potato, and especially, it seems, in the Church. Repeatedly questions like 'Why does it seem the Church is only interested in my money?' and 'Is it OK for Christians to be rich?' are asked. We'll also engage head-on with the modern-day thinking that some have propagated – that if you give more freely, God will automatically reward you by making you rich. Could these questions and thinking arise because there is so much more to it than money itself? We will discover that money is a major player for the enemy and it has a stronger hold over us than we realize. Actually, the *Bible* speaks about money more often than about faith. God apparently isn't shy about broaching the subject as a breakthrough in this area will instigate a breakthrough in so much more.

As you read through the chapters of this book, you'll discover a fresh way to see the plan God has for your future. You'll discover a pathway to become debt free and release an ability to live generously while also creating a personal future of more than enough. God wants each one of us to enjoy abundance, but financial breakthrough is based on a lot more than just increasing our giving.

> Financial breakthrough is based on a lot more than just increasing our giving

## FINANCIAL BREAKTHROUGH ATTRACTS ATTENTION

Have you ever wondered why, when a church grows and becomes of significant influence, the first thing the media attack almost always relates to money? We've all seen it in the news. The stories that appear about the house a pastor lives in or the car they drive. The articles are seldom ever factual and usually succeed in promoting a roaring suspicion about the integrity of the particular leader's motives. Even though there is very little concrete evidence available, judgements are made about that person and some of it sticks and questions remain.

I'm not saying some Christian leaders don't make mistakes; at times the way money has been handled in the church environment has been completely unethical. But have you ever asked yourself why these types of stories are so common? I think there's a fairly simple answer, although for many it may be just as controversial as the whole topic of God and money. It is my conviction that it is because the devil knows that when we break through materially and live an expanding kingdom future, we will become an agent of incredible good. It's there for all to see in God's word, clearly stated:

**Proverbs 11:10-11** *When it goes well with the righteous, the city rejoices; and when the wicked perish, there is jubilation. By the blessing of the upright the city is exalted, but it is overthrown by the mouth of the wicked.*

---

**Either you direct money or money will direct you**

---

In *God Money & Me* we are going to tackle this topic that is possibly our number-one ongoing life challenge: either you direct money or money will direct you.

## CHALLENGING WRONG THINKING

I grew up in the Church, and without even knowing it, for the greater part of my life I was only taught the law of sowing and living generously. I don't for a moment challenge what was being taught but I discovered this was not enough to create a financial pathway; in fact, in isolation from other biblical principles regarding money, it ended up being a very narrow view.

The enemy has a goal and that is to restrict our ability to break through in this area so he can suppress the purposes of God. As we have already seen in *Proverbs 11*, even a city is better off when things go well for the righteous.

When we realize that God has called us to live a blessed life and we live out that blessing, even the city we live in is elevated. *Proverbs* continues to teach us, however, that limitations result when we accept the intimidation of a lying enemy.

When you look at the phrase 'the blessing of the upright' in *Proverbs 11*, the word 'blessing' in the original means the 'prosperity' or the 'liberal pool' of the upright. In other words, if God could take your life and my life and create a liberal pool, we would become part of the answer, not part of the problem.

Obviously, the exhortation and teaching found in *God Money & Me* will be unapologetic in the way it talks about money. I believe that God is going to challenge each one of us to align our human response to His purpose. For many of us it may be the first time we've had our hearts exposed to truths about the power and the influence of mammon.

We will examine how money in itself is neither good nor bad, but it does have a righteous or corrupted power attached to it. And by God's grace we're going to construct a financial foundation that will provide for the purposes of God in and through our lives.

## DISTRACTED BY MONEY?

We've already mentioned the very high levels of relational discord, from arguments to divorce, that money causes. Also, I would suggest to you from personal experience and observation that as many as 80 to 90 percent of Christians are bound by a lack of money or distracted by the unsurrendered power of it.

> 80 to 90 percent of Christians are bound by a lack of money or distracted by the unsurrendered power of it

And yet somehow within the Church, it's somewhat taboo to go there. We avoid monetary conversations because of the impending reaction. And when we have broached the subject, it seems that all too often we have significantly missed the mark with teaching that is shallow, superficial and unable to empower us to create a financial pathway. Let's go back to the beginning of time:

*Genesis 1:27-28 So God created man in His own image; in the image of God He created him; male and female He created them. Then God blessed them, and God said to them, 'Be fruitful and multiply; fill the earth and subdue it; have dominion over the fish of the sea, over the birds of the air, and over every living thing that moves on the earth.'*

Think about that. The *Bible* says that God created you, He created me, in His own image. And then He blessed us. God blessed us. He said: 'Understanding that you are blessed, now YOU are to become fruitful, multiply, fill the earth and subdue the earth. And then have dominion over the things that I've created' (paraphrased).

On my journey to discovering the pathway to financial freedom, I began to ponder seriously why for so long I felt it was wrong to break through into blessing and why others seemed to judge me when I did, even though it had always been God's intent. Early on as a pastor, I can remember being overwhelmed and so influenced by other people's opinions. One particular day, I recall wearing a new shirt that I had found in an amazing sale. At the time, Maree and I were only at the beginning of our journey of discovery into understanding that God wants us to break through in blessing. A church member came up and said, 'Oh, nice shirt – is it new?' I immediately responded, 'Well, yes, but I bought it in a sale.' Looking back, it wasn't that the church member's question was wrong, but it was the tone and the spirit it came with. It felt like they were saying, 'you shouldn't have enough money to buy a new shirt if you are a real pastor.' It was a long time ago, but it left me feeling guilty.

If we don't understand that we were blessed at the beginning, then we're not going to unlock that blessing today. We're not going to commit to multiplying our lives. We're definitely not going to entertain having dominion over our resources and future.

> If we don't understand that we were blessed at the beginning, then we're not going to unlock that blessing today

So, a key principle when we think about *God Money & Me* is to grasp this foundational truth. It will require the reprogramming of our souls and minds until it becomes a revelation.

## BE FRUITFUL AND MULTIPLY

I was created to be fruitful, to multiply and to have dominion.

That is something to get excited about! You may not be jumping up and down quite yet, but once you really understand this, you will! I've had to shift my own mind-set over and over again. If God created me and blessed me, if I am called to be fruitful and to multiply, and I am not experiencing more breakthrough than five years ago, there's something that needs to be confronted and changed. If I was called to have dominion over the things that seek to reduce and limit me, I need to address wrong thinking and the enemy's lies that have lodged in my mind, and say to my now and to my future, 'Devil, you will have no say-so.'

The New Testament underscores this view in *Matthew 25*, with the Parable of the Talents. Three servants are highlighted. One had five talents, one had two, one had one. The one who was rebuked by the master was the one who didn't multiply what he had. He was loyal, but didn't multiply. True faithfulness, according to this passage, is the combination of loyalty and fruitfulness.

My own story perfectly reflects this confusion we've had

concerning our understanding of the proper use of our money. My wife Maree and I started our married life together at the age of 23. Soon after paying off our wedding, we started saving for a deposit on a house. However, we continually became aware of either a need in someone's personal situation or the Church's financial needs. We completely understood what generosity looked like – we believed in the law of sowing and simply loved to give.

On several occasions, we actually gave all our savings away. I remember turning 38, 15 years later, and all of a sudden stopping and realizing after all our giving, we still didn't have a home of our own or even a deposit to buy one. Nobody ever said to me, 'Paul, you know what? Your life should be a generous life, but your life is not just about giving everything away.' In fact, most of the preaching we heard in Church around money was only about the sowing of our seed.

Yes, there is no doubt that God has called us to be a generous, giving people. But I had to re-learn, to re-study the *Bible* and to understand with greater clarity the full economic principle of sowing and reaping. You see, we had embraced the law of sowing, but never understood the law of reaping. You may find yourself exactly where Maree and I were, but the good news is that this first revelation changes everything. It is only through doing both – sowing and reaping – that we increase our ability to live a 'larger life pool' and create a balanced financial life.

> We had embraced the law of sowing, but never understood the law of reaping

## DOMINATED BY DEBT
**2 Corinthians 9:8** *And God is able to make all grace abound toward you...*

You may feel there is little hope for your future financial world because your life has been dominated by debt. Did you know that the *Bible* has an answer to break that domination? You are not a special case. You may say, 'I've been in poverty for years; there seems to be no hope for me.' There is hope for you. God is able. Our breakthrough requires a personal revelation from God's word! *2 Corinthians* continues: '... *that you, always having all sufficiency in all things...*'.

It is amazing how many have echoed that over the years. 'Yeah, that's it; see, Pastor, you need to watch out for that prosperity thinking, because all we need is sufficiency.' The *Bible* says we need sufficiency in all things: not just in our day-to-day needs but also in all things. Enough to provide an answer to the needs of the community we're in and have the ability to feed the poor, fund God's purpose, and do a list of other things that could fill this entire book. Do you have sufficiency for that? If you have a problem with that, let's go on with the verse: '... *[that you] may have an abundance for every good work.*'

How many of us are in a place where, no matter where we went in the world, no matter who came across our path, no matter who knocked on our door, we would have an abundance available to help? As I've contended for years, if we don't, I don't think we've seen the promise fulfilled yet. This word 'grace' means God is able to make all favor, all liberality come towards us, that we may have all sufficiency – literally a perfect condition of life, in which we need no aid or external benefit.

As Christians, we should be living at a level most of us haven't experienced yet. A place where we are in the driver's seat over every decision that once was determined by money. It will not happen overnight – quite possibly, it will take a committed season of right response – but ultimately God's plan is to have money serve us, not us serve money.

---

**God's plan is to have money serve us, not us serve money**

---

When Christians fail to actually understand what God has said and allow wrong thinking to stifle their expectations, the purposes of God are limited. But *2 Corinthians 9:8* promises that, as believers, we should have an abundance, we should have an excess in quality and quantity, that we will excel, and that we will live over and above financial restriction.

If this is true, if this is God's word, we have to say: 'Wow! I've got to change something.'

## LIVING THE CHALLENGE

Have you had a chance to accept and digest what I've just been saying? You were and are created to be fruitful, to multiply and to have dominion. That is the challenge we are given. Where are you at in light of this today?

You might say, 'Paul, that's a bit strong.' Well, I'm sorry; I'm going to give the devil whatever I can give him over the rest of this teaching to empower God's people to be fruitful and multiply. You see, when we react to correct teaching on money, it reflects the state of our heart. And before you say you're not that comfortable with too much talk about money, think about this:

- If you love marriage, you'll love teaching on building relational strength.
- If you love winning people to Christ, you'll love teaching on evangelism.
- If you love generosity, you'll love teaching on financial breakthrough.

We've already established that money is a very powerful, influential commodity that has the ability to generate suspicion and misunderstanding.

- People say, 'Money can't make you happy.'
  No, but it can make life a lot more pleasant.
- You tell your kids, 'Money doesn't grow on trees.'
  No, it comes from your parents' pockets.
- 'Well, money's not the ultimate answer.'
  No, but it does provide a lot of answers to a lot of people.

*New York Times* best-selling author and influential financial coach Robert G. Allen has said, 'Money is one of the most important subjects to study in your entire life. Some of life's greatest enjoyments and most of life's greatest disappointments stem from the decisions you make about money. Whether you experience great peace of mind or constant anxiety will depend on whether you get your finances under control.'

In the next section, we'll examine some of the Eight Common Myths about money. You may find out that a lot of what you think you know about money just 'isn't true' at all – that's the good news.

# TWO

# MONEY'S MISUNDERSTOOD AUTHORITY

---

I think you'd have to agree that money in our earthly existence is one of life's most powerful forces. Ask yourself: 'How much of my daily, weekly and annual activities are influenced by money?' Personally, it was a shock to me when I discovered how much of my thinking on the topic was simply untrue and unbalanced. I was influenced by 'myths' that do not stand up under the searchlight of scripture. I'd suggest these 'myths' are often so deeply ingrained in our thinking that we accept them as 'facts of life' without ever taking a closer look at how they line up with God's word.

---

> How we use money demonstrates the reality of our love for God

As Charles Caldwell Ryrie says in *Balancing the Christian Life*, 'How we use money demonstrates the reality of our love for God. In some ways it proves our love more conclusively than depth of knowledge, length of prayers or prominence of service. The use of our possessions shows us up for what we actually are.' The *Bible* is not ambiguous on the importance money plays in our lives. From as far back as King Solomon we are reminded in **Ecclesiastes 10:19:** *'A feast is made for laughter, and wine makes merry; but money answers everything.'*

Think about it:
- Money says to debt, 'I can free you.'
- Money says to vision, 'I can release you.'
- Money says to time, 'I can direct you.'
- Money says to need, 'I can help you.'

To help you gain an insight into the role money plays, in this chapter we will begin to unravel the first two of Eight Money Myths that incorrectly navigate our thinking when it comes to monetary wealth.

## MYTH ONE – 'MONEY IS NOT SOMETHING WE SHOULD FOCUS ON'

Many people, without even knowing it, think we shouldn't focus on money. My question is, 'Well, why not?' If money is what decides how and where we live, if money determines what we do with our future, if money controls where we work, if money brings an answer to those in need, why wouldn't we talk about it? Money is arguably one of our world's most powerful agents.

> **Money is arguably one of our world's most powerful agents**

**Proverbs 22:7** *The rich rules over the poor, and the borrower is servant to the lender.*

In other words, if you're in a place where you're in debt that is unsustainable, you are no longer in a place of freedom.

Money can release so much but, equally, when we find ourselves under its power, we end up living in a place of restriction and at times overwhelming domination. Jesus constantly warned about wrong lordship, and once again satan uses money to seek to control us. I am fully convinced that God has a way for each one of us to regain the place of financial freedom.

Here is a challenging question: What percentage of Christians do you think are living under the domination of money? Believe it or not, I would say in excess of 80 percent. By saying domination, I am implying that they are not in a place of release from the restrictions that money places over them. Even those who have money often fall into the trap of living distractedly, allowing it to hinder them from making kingdom-centered decisions.

> We can't afford to allow material circumstances to control our life-defining decisions

So, whether we like it or not, whether we are struggling financially or are living comfortably, we can't afford to allow material circumstances to control our life-defining decisions. What do we find if we look to scripture for guidance on our thinking here?

## THE BIBLE TALKS ABOUT MONEY MORE THAN FAITH

You may have doubted the statement I made in the previous chapter about there being more verses on money than on either faith or salvation. So, just for the record, there are 215 pertaining to faith, 218 to salvation, and 2,058 dealing with stewardship and accountability with regard to money. Don't get me wrong – the importance of our faith is number one, but it is time for us to uncover the keys to financial freedom through His word.

I went online some time ago and read about world debt. Did you know that world debt, last time I looked, was in excess of $58,000,000,000,000. That's over $58 trillion. I watched the clock, and in less than two minutes, it had gone up another $10 million, because of accumulating debt interest. Doesn't that fill you with anticipation about the financial future of the planet? No, I didn't think so. Do you still think we shouldn't talk about money?

When we consider King Solomon's reflection on money in *Ecclesiastes*, and his conclusion that it 'answers everything', where does that leave us? It should bring us to the realization that this is 'King Solomon', in all his wisdom, in essence saying that we're living in a natural world that has a lot more to do with money than we would ever dare to consider.

We must take care that we don't become settled and satisfied with just meeting our own needs when it comes to our finances. I have discovered that this kind of thinking reflects a very me-centered world view. Jesus taught that we were to be His answer to a world in need and if we embrace that mission and mandate, then our thinking must come into line with living out of abundance. It's a Money Myth that we don't need to talk about money.

**MYTH TWO – 'GOD'S BLESSINGS ARE NOT MATERIAL'**
As mentioned earlier, I have been in the Church my entire life and have heard some of the craziest teachings. One example is that God's blessing is limited to spiritual blessing. In a conversation I once had, I was told, 'God is a blessing God; yes, I accept that. But it is spiritual blessing that He guarantees us, not material blessing.' This myth needs to come into line with scriptural thinking.

**John 10:10** *The thief does not come except to steal, and to kill, and to destroy. I have come that they may have life, and that they may have it more abundantly.*

Think about that verse: The thief comes to steal, kill and destroy. Satan wants to take everything of God's promised enlargement and reduce it to nothing. Jesus says that He has come so that we may have life, and that life would be abundant. The original word for 'life' is 'zōē'. It's Greek, and stands for the perfect state of living, where you have need of nothing. Again, another WOW.

God is effectively telling us: 'When I created you, I blessed you. And I called you to embrace a thinking that says you're fruitful, you're going to multiply, you're going to have dominion.' The word 'abundantly' in *John 10:10* translates as 'to be exceeding beyond measure, superior and extraordinary, remarkable, eminent, more excellent'.

## When I created you, I blessed you

This is not some self-focused, me-first prosperity preacher speaking but an eternal, everlasting, all-able God promising that, in everything, we were born to overcome and become more than conquerors. Why, then, do we restrict our expectations? Knowing we have the God of limitless ability living within and stirring our hearts, we can't help but be challenged to think differently. Ask God to renew your mind, because you were created to be fruitful: to multiply and have dominion.

I remember in my earlier ministry years preaching at a Christian music festival in New Zealand, and I felt to speak on *3 John 2*, which presents these incredible words:

*3 John 2 Beloved, I pray that you may prosper in all things and be in health, just as your soul prospers.*

You would not believe the unexpected storm of disapproving emails I received in response to that message, from people across many different churches. 'How disgusting. You prosperity preacher...'

they wrote, 'That you would try to put that money carrot before people.' Even back then, I realized that in our nation of New Zealand, we had such a limited, small, wrong understanding in regard to God's desire to see blessing in and through us. And I'm not confident a whole lot has changed in the mind-sets of many of God's children today.

**Prosperity is not a dirty word but a Biblical concept that frees us to be able to free others**

When you develop a prosperous heart, everything about your life becomes prosperous. And yet God doesn't want to make you prosperous beyond the size of your heart's ability to understand and to use your prosperity in His way. And so, prosperity is not just about being blessed for blessing's sake – if that's our motive, we'll trip over ourselves and fall into the trap that unsurrendered money can create. Prosperity is not a dirty word, but a biblical concept that frees us to be able to free others. The facts are that when the big ME gets in the way in anything, everything about us becomes imbalanced.

## PROSPERITY REQUIRES AN ENLARGED HEART
Maybe today you are where I was many years ago, when I said, 'God, I believe Your word but it is just not happening. Show me what needs to change.' I want to emphasize again that all of us have an unlimited God who wants to breathe His love and abundance into our lives. The challenge is that this truth is most often lost between the presentation of two extremes.

After visiting the Netherlands some years ago, the country of my parents' birth, I was amazed by how religious this nation had been. It's a land where so much of a belief in God has ended up in legalism. Yet you go to Amsterdam, and all around you is an overt expression of liberalism. The Holy Spirit nudged me to stop and consider the two extremes. When the Church becomes stuck in legalism, people rebel and end in liberalism. What is needed is coming back to the liberty that true freedom brings. Biblical blessing lives between the two extremes of lack and unsurrendered excess.

> **Biblical blessing lives between the two extremes of lack and unsurrendered excess**

Prosperity is not a case of, 'If you do this, you'll be blessed and have whatever you want whenever you want it.' Instead, it is when your heart becomes enlarged with truth and commits to activate the will and purposes of God in material things. I wish I had understood this a whole lot earlier.

*Proverbs 10:22 The blessing of the LORD makes one rich, and He adds no sorrow with it.*

You might wonder if we're talking about material blessing – and yes, the original word for 'rich' translates as rich in every sphere of living, including money and material things. Not only that, but 'He adds no sorrow with it'. It's not contrived; it's not ill-gotten. I love what John D. Rockefeller, who during his lifetime was one of the world's wealthiest men and a major philanthropist, said: 'God gave me my money. I believe the power to make money is a gift from God. It is to be developed and used to the best of our ability, for the good of mankind. Having been endowed with the gift I possess, I believe it is my duty to make money and still more money, and to use the money I make for the good of my fellow man according to the dictates of my conscience.' (Rockefeller's faith was the guiding force of his life and he believed it to be the source of his success.)

Let's continue on to deal with Myth Three – one of the greatest myths of all time – that the *Bible* says money is evil. If you believe that then I've got news for you!

THREE

# MONEY'S NOT EVIL

---

Hillsong's Pastor Brian Houston heads one of the most vibrant international ministries on the planet, now meeting in more than 80 locations across 17 countries (at the time of writing), with weekly attendances of well in excess of 90,000 people. Hillsong choruses are sung in churches all around the world. Yet when he was recounting, at the 2015 Sydney Hillsong Conference, what he considered the 'wins' and 'failures' Hillsong had seen to the Body of Christ, he dwelt on an initiative he said he'd quickly come to regret: he had titled the first book he ever wrote *You Need More Money*. That seems harmless enough to me because of the revelation I now carry and also because, having grown up with Pastor Brian and being a lifelong friend of his, I can vouch for the integrity of his heart. After all, who among us would not acknowledge that having more money would be more than welcome? But in the kingdom of God it's not that simple. Pastor Brian confided to the many thousands assembled that he hadn't realized 'you had to be either brave or foolhardy to write a book titled like that'.

At the time, he was bombarded from within the Church, and from outside the Church, with very definite messages about how inappropriate it was for a pastor to suggest we might want to be more fruitful (my term)! Yet I was sitting there in the stadium, hand on heart, thinking, 'Brian, that was a brilliant thing you did', and because of it, I was encouraged to go on my own search for financial freedom.

The very strong response Pastor Brian received from many well-intended and other not-so-well-intended people can often be based around Myth Three. It's the mistaken belief that money is evil. So, let's examine that more closely.

## MYTH THREE – 'BUT THE BIBLE TEACHES MONEY IS EVIL'

Again, I ask, who told you that? The power of money can destroy, certainly. But it also builds.

> The power of money can destroy, certainly. But it also builds

The Church can be likened to the beautiful coconut trees that grow on some of the Pacific Islands. I have visited the Islands many times and the beauty is beyond belief as these magnificent trees line the coastal fringe. As you look closer, you discover many have grown with a real bend, due to a high-wind environment. And so they have ended up unable to display their full beauty.

This is a picture of us as the Church when we've allowed myths about money to define us. We feel guilty if we try to stand tall and say, 'You know what? The blessing of God is on me.' And so, we end up cowering to the pressure of what the world and many ill-informed, religious-minded people would say.

I believe the Church is the best agent globally to steward the most resources to accomplish the greatest work in assisting the growing real community need around us.

We need more money! If we really have the King's heart, that seemingly controversial statement is exactly right. It's not just about us. It's also about the blessing that will flow through us. We have gone so far the other way that we have allowed the enemy and the isolated misdemeanors of a few misguided people to stop us from stepping into what God has promised.

Have you ever realized that a fire is wonderfully useful when it is positioned in a fireplace? What does it do? It warms the home. It contributes to an inviting atmosphere in the home. But if you set that fire outside the fireplace, it will destroy your home. This is also true with money. It does have the power to destroy us, but when understood and handled correctly, it can release God's purpose through us.

> You can't change the world without the resources needed

Why would we allow a few excesses, and those who have done the wrong thing by manipulating events for their own ends within the Church, to take us to this point where we think that all money is evil? You say you want to change the world. Well, you can't change the world without the resources needed.

## FOR THE LOVE OF MONEY

Money is not evil. The verse that is most often misquoted on this is found in the book of *1 Timothy*.

*1 Timothy 6:10 For the love of money is a root of all kinds of evil, for which some have strayed from the faith in their greediness, and pierced themselves through with many sorrows.*

It's the 'love' of money, not money itself, that produces evil. When you have to have money, your life is all about you – you have succumbed to loving money. I've seen people over the years bury themselves in the security they think provisions can bring. Ultimately they almost always end up stranded. They may love God and want to fulfill His purposes, yet they become controlled by money when they are seduced to make it the source of their focus, love and eventually worship. They wouldn't identify it as the love of money, but it's their decision-maker and ultimately their security. If we live for money, we will end up straying from God's purposes.

**1 Timothy 6:6** *Now godliness with contentment is great gain.*

People argue that this statement means we shouldn't be believing for more and the gain is non-material. Never isolate a scripture outside of the tenor of God's word on the whole picture. No, money is not evil. The love of money is evil. Some may say, 'but all we need is contentment, and with contentment is great gain.' True, but the verse reads godliness with contentment. Godliness is God in His fullness, His purposes living fully formed in and through me.

'But money changes you,' you say. 'Does it?' I'd contend that money doesn't so much change you as unmask the real you. If your heart isn't fully surrendered and submitted to God at its core, money can cause great damage, but it's not evil. Money is simply a provision, to be used for good.

> ## Money doesn't so much change you as unmask the real you

## A GOOD SERVANT BUT A BAD MASTER

I love this quote from French author Alexandre Dumas: 'Do not value money for any more nor any less than it's worth; it is a good servant but a bad master.' That's worth remembering: money is a good servant but a bad master.

Casey Treat, a good friend of mine and a co-founder with his wife Wendy of the Christian Faith Center in Seattle, gave me a really helpful example from his own life a few years ago. A kinda religious person came up to Pastor Casey and said, 'Oh, what a beautiful tie. Silk, is it?' This person then had the audacity to lift the tie, look at the label and then comment, 'Oh, very expensive'. Pastor Casey told me he just looked at the person and replied, 'Actually, it's just worm-vomit'. Did you know that's how silk is made? Perfect way to bring some perspective.

I'm trying my best here to make my point loud and clear that money's not evil. It's the love of money that's evil. Take a moment to remind yourself: I was created to be fruitful, I was created to multiply, and I was created by God to have dominion. Microsoft founder Bill Gates made a lot of money from being co-founder of the world's biggest computer software company. But I love the day I heard he had donated more than $28 billion to charity (and so, I am sure, do those who were the beneficiaries).

Don't tell me that money is evil. The LOVE OF MONEY is evil. I get a lot of pleasure out of quoting the following:

**1 Timothy 6:17** *Instruct those who are rich in this present world not to be conceited or to fix their hope on the uncertainty of riches, but on God who richly supplies us with all things to enjoy.* (NASB)

Do you get that? It's the heart of the Father. God wants to do us good and because of Him we can believe for so much more.

'Hang on a minute,' you might say. 'OK, you've convinced me money is not itself evil, but the love of money is. Yet didn't Jesus live the life of a poor carpenter? Didn't Jesus model a life of scarcity? And what about all the great saints who've gone before, like St

> **God wants to do us good and because of Him we can believe for so much more**

Francis of Assisi or Nobel Peace Prize winner Mother Teresa? Isn't it something "everybody knows" – that true holiness is found in a life of poverty, not wealth?'

Glad you asked. That takes us right on to Myth Four.

# FOUR

# ABUNDANT SUPPLY

---

Google the phrase 'Christians and money' and you'll find at least half of the entries show just how uncomfortable believers are with dealing with the concept that we are to live with financial significance, having enough money to be able to bring an answer. Coming near the top of the list of entries are headlines like, 'Fellow Christians, I'm Rich and I'm Sorry'. So, let's ask the question: 'Can Christians be rich and faithful as well?'

## MYTH FOUR – 'JESUS MODELED SCARCITY'
Didn't Jesus live a very meager kind of life, and wasn't the gospel He represented one of frugal living?

I think many of us have been subjected to this view of the gospel over the years. We've heard stories of internationally-recognized Christians like Mother Teresa, who served the dying poor in Calcutta (now Kolkata). We think about how she forfeited personal needs as part of her calling for the purposes of God. That seems to be brought automatically to the fore as the model for true holiness.

There's no doubt that God has special missions for some people, and who can argue that the call over Mother Teresa's life was powerful and full of supernatural breakthrough? But this doesn't mean that all of us are meant to live with nothing, because if we were all like Mother Teresa, no one would have had the financial resources to fund her work and help meet the vast needs she found herself surrounded by.

Mother Teresa was never shy in validating the need for money to alleviate suffering. Among the many dozens of missions she founded globally was a small one in Port-au-Prince, Haiti, one of the world's most desperately poor places. A day after Mother Teresa visited there, the daughter-in-law of the hated Haitian dictator Jean-Claude 'Baby Doc' Duvalier, who was accused of murdering thousands of his political opponents, went to Mother Teresa's mission and donated $1,000. Not a million, as some of her more vocal critics claimed. But why did she accept it, the accusers asked. It was blood money, dirty money. Her answer was concise. In charity, she said, everyone has a right to give. 'I have no right to judge them. God alone has that right. . . I do not ask for money. But people have a right to give.'

## Money provides an answer for need

Once again, money provides an answer for need.

## SORRY, GOT IT WRONG

And then there are some who've chosen to turn that idea really on its head and claim Jesus was rich. I've heard preachers say, 'Well, Jesus wasn't really without money. In fact, He was very rich. Remember the garments He had on when He was crucified? They were regarded as so desirable that the soldiers cast lots for them' *(Mark 15:24)*. I don't think that proves He had a lot of money. I'm sure somebody may have given Him some beautiful garments and many invested in His ministry, but to stretch that to being rich is excessive.

The truth is, Jesus modeled a life of having few human possessions. The question is, was there a reason for that? I think we find the answer below.

**2 Corinthians 8:9** *For you know the grace of our Lord Jesus Christ, that though He was rich, yet for your sakes He became poor, that you through His poverty might become rich.*

It's so important that you get a hold of this verse because it unlocks a lot of incorrect mind-sets around living a blessed life. 'Though He was rich.' The original denotes not just spiritual riches but so much more. It simply means, 'Though He had all of heaven at His disposal, He left it all to create a way that we could experience blessing in every part of our lives – spirit, soul and body.'

'Though He was rich, yet for your sakes He became poor...' for you, for me, right now. 'He became poor, that you through His poverty might become rich.' I have no doubt this includes natural resources. That word 'rich' means 'abounding in material sources' – abundantly supplied. I think you can match this verse back to the following one:

**2 Corinthians 9:8** *God is able to make all grace abound toward you, that you, always having all sufficiency in all things, may have an abundance for every good work.*

This is a defining point, because if we don't accept that God has created us to live materially blessed, our thinking will ultimately limit us. For many years, as I have mentioned, when God blessed me in a material way, I felt extremely embarrassed and didn't know how to respond. This helped me a lot. God says it is fine for you to have stuff; just don't let that stuff have you.

**God says it is fine for you to have stuff: just don't let that stuff have you**

When the purposes of the King are at the base of who we are, we become recipients of His kingdom. Why would we cause His life and what Jesus did for us to be of no effect in this area because of a wrong understanding? The fact is, according to scripture, that we will all be in awe once we see the wonder of heaven (what some would call opulence). Creation gives us a foretaste. Also remember that Jesus always showed that when God became involved, there was an abundance through His ministry. Whenever Jesus performed a miracle, He never did just enough: He always brought abundant supply (like feeding the 5,000, with 12 basketfuls remaining).

## WHAT ABOUT THE DISCIPLES

Jesus sent the disciples out with nothing, very true. Many times God will allow us, and indeed require us, to have seasons of complete reliance on Him. His blessing plan is not a blanket guarantee that we will have material provision in every season. In *Matthew 10:8-10*, for example, when Jesus sent the 12 disciples out to 'heal the sick, raise the dead, cleanse those who have leprosy, drive out demons' (NIV), He told them:

*Matthew 10:8-10 Freely you have received; freely give. Do not get any gold or silver or copper to take with you in your belts – no bag for the journey or extra shirt or sandals or a staff, for the worker is worth his keep. (NIV)*

Jesus was preparing them for the beginning of their ministry life. Effective ministry – and, in fact, every day Christianity – requires that we learn how to trust God and live by faith. There will be times in our lives when we're asking God where the blessing is and God will be saying, 'You've got to trust Me. You've got to have faith in My word.' These seasons always create a greater depth of relationship and dependence.

However, we'd be wrong to argue that everyone who is truly living a committed ministry life should go with nothing and never see a breakthrough in the area of provision. Compare these two passages below:

**Luke 22:35-36** *'When I sent you without purse, bag or sandals, did you lack anything?' 'Nothing,' they answered. He said to them, 'But now if you have a purse, take it, and also a bag; and if you don't have a sword, sell your cloak and buy one'.* (NIV)

**Mark 10:29-30** *Assuredly, I say to you, there is no one who has left house or brothers or sisters or father or mother or wife or children or lands, for My sake and the gospel's, who shall not receive a hundredfold now in this time – houses and brothers and sisters and mothers and children and lands, with persecutions – and in the age to come, eternal life.*

Jesus did not preach a gospel of scarcity. He modeled a life of going without, so that you and I could step up into the promise of abundance, providing an answer for the world in which we live.

And it doesn't matter where we find ourselves right now: when it comes to money, we don't have to stay there; but change begins on a foundation of right biblical understanding mixed with an obedient response. We've got to go into this week, our next month, and the rest of this year with the revelation that we were created to be fruitful; we were created to multiply. If we're not multiplying, there's something wrong. And we were created to have dominion. So, even if

> Change begins on a foundation of right biblical understanding mixed with an obedient response

we've lived under the curse of debt, it's time for us to realize we have dominion over debt. Allow the truth of this to penetrate deep into your soul.

## THE TEST OF THE SILVER COMMODORE

Let me tell you a story that comes out of my personal experience. I grew up in a good church, but, as I've said, any teaching we had about money was all about giving – about sowing, but not about reaping. I often say to people today that I had a theology of sowing but not of reaping.

I had just bought a replacement car. It was a silver Commodore, well used and second-hand – there, I'm justifying myself again. And I was feeling a little self-conscious, wondering what the people in Church were going to think about it, as it was better than my previous car, a little four-door gold Honda.

I just happened to hear an evangelist preaching passionately about a great truth in the kingdom, from *Luke 14:28*, on the cost of being a disciple. In it, Jesus says that if you do not forsake all that you have, you cannot be His disciple. Discussing this passage, the preacher posed an interesting question: 'Why would you spend 10, 12, 15, 20, 50 thousand dollars on a car, when you could buy one for $2,000 that would do exactly the same job: drive you forward and drive you back?' He said if you bought the $2,000 car, you would be in a position to invest the rest of the money into ministry.

Straightaway I felt condemnation swell up within. We had just spent $11,000 on the silver Commodore, which at the time was quite a stretch. We were beginning to believe that God had no problem about us being blessed, because we had been blessing others. I will never forget how confused I felt after that message. My sensitive heart straightaway responded: 'did we miss God in buying it?' Deep in the midst of mixed emotions, I'll never forget what happened the following week. I was on the Auckland motorway, pondering all of this. I was battling feelings of confusion and guilt when, all of a sudden, I found myself tailing a brand-new red HSV Commodore. There was my ultimate dream car, new paint sparkling in the sunshine. The deep rumble of the exhaust could be heard by all those around. Then I saw the number plate. Believe it or not, it was 'ELSDAI', which I understood to mean El Shaddai, a name of God that means 'I will provide'.

I had just been saying to God, 'Is it wrong to own an $11,000 car?' Then I catch sight of this new red HSV with the number plate 'I will provide'. Again I was reminded that sometimes God does lead us to go without for a greater purpose, but righteous living is not about living small. Surrendered, yes, but limited, no.

> **Righteous living is not about living small**

I began to echo, 'I was created to be fruitful, to multiply, to have dominion.' I didn't use those exact words, but it was as if God challenged: 'Hey, son, you've lived with a "pool" image. There's only so much water in the pool. I'm not a pool, I'm a river. There's so much more.' It was a turning point for me, and I hope, if you can grasp it, it will be for you, too. If the enemy can keep you and me small, he's also going to keep our kingdom impact small. Remember, Jesus taught the disciples to pray, 'Your kingdom come on earth as it is in heaven.'

## GOD'S PROVISION IS MAGNANIMOUS

Perhaps you are starting to get some inkling of how great God's purpose for provision truly is. He is not the God of limited supply and He can never give too much or ever run out. No! He is an endless river. His bounty is shown throughout His creation.

Some people, when talking of some church property, say, 'It's too opulent.' If that is the case, we are going to feel very uncomfortable when we get to heaven, where, we are told, there is silver, gold and precious stones. God doesn't see it as opulence. He's the God who owns the cattle on a thousand hills; He's the God who speaks things into existence.

Misdirected thinking produces comments such as 'Well, I'm not going to that church; they spent too much on the foyer.' Here in New Zealand some ask the question, 'Have you ever been to that LIFE church? They have real commercial coffee machines; such a waste.' I don't know about you, but a little good coffee increases my anointing, ha-ha. Seriously, let's challenge all small thinking that seeks to attach itself to us.

I love something 18th-century British theologian John Wesley said: 'You need to earn all you can. You need to save all you can. You need to give all you can.' It's not just one paradigm: it's earning, saving, giving. It's building a future.

## Earn all you can, save all you can, give all you can

We're here to set up a platform for the generations to come.

That leads us to a consideration of the next very important wrong understanding about money and *Bible* teaching: Myth Five – 'God's kingdom doesn't need my money.' How wrong can we be?

FIVE

# BUILDING GOD'S KINGDOM

More than at any other time in history, I believe now is the season for the Church to rise and make a difference in the cities we live in. Our secular arena does not have many answers to the economic challenges our world faces, but the *Bible* promises that if we engage God's blessings, our cities will be all the better for it. Remember what we've already found in Chapter 1 in relation to a flourishing city life:

*Proverbs 11:10-11 When it goes well with the righteous, the city rejoices; and when the wicked perish, there is jubilation. By the blessing of the upright the city is exalted, but it is overthrown by the mouth of the wicked.*

We are called to be salt and light, fulfilling our purpose to affect those around us with good. How we release and manage our resources has a lot to do with impacting those around us.

This is our time to bring God's goodness to people. The fact is that we never arrive and there is always so much more. Sometimes I think we have a picture of heaven as something static, but my understanding of heaven is that it's dynamic – God is continuing to unfold His multifaceted glory to His creation through all of time. God has no limitations. God does not get to the end of Himself. God is everlasting. The point is that you and I were designed in the image of God; therefore, let's never park at where we find ourselves today.

## Let's never park at where we find ourselves today

God created us to live His promised reflection: 'Our future is filled with so much more.' Why not make this our catch-cry in the next season of life?

Whatever is standing in the way of our breakthrough, we have the right to see change in all areas of living and especially in the area of finances. How can we bring a blessing in an area we are not blessed in? As Jesus said, if you see a man on the street cold and naked, don't just pray for him, also give him a meal and a coat.

THE GOSPEL OF 'JUST ENOUGH'
Look at the prayer King David offered up when he was leading the people in presenting their offerings at the temple of God:

*1 Chronicles 29:12 Both riches and honor come from You, and You reign over all. In Your hand is power and might; in Your hand it is to make great and to give strength to all.*

Many of us drift in our walk of faith. Because of setbacks, hurts and disappointments in life, we look at what has been or what's gone wrong and we settle, simply hoping to survive. We can so easily end up living by a gospel of 'just enough'.

But God is saying, 'Don't be like that. Realize I'm the God who can bring any breakthrough, as long as you're prepared to carry it in a kingdom way. I'm committed to preparing and offering a depth of understanding so you don't get sidelined when the goodness of God comes to you.'

In previous chapters, we've examined some of the myths that lead to wrong thinking. Maybe you're ready to acknowledge that, whether you like it or not, for most of us money consumes most of who we are in some way. So, let's move on with uncovering a few more of the many myths that keep us locked out of God's purposes.

### MYTH FIVE – 'GOD'S KINGDOM DOESN'T NEED MONEY'

We need to understand that money isn't the thing that should rule us; however, we can release the kingdom by the correct use of it. In the Lord's prayer, we declare, 'Your kingdom come'. Come where? On earth? How's that going to happen? How will that take place if we continue with a lack of supply?

> **We can release the kingdom by the correct use of money**

*Luke 11:2 So He said to them, 'When you pray, say: "Our Father in heaven, hallowed be Your name. Your kingdom come. Your will be done on earth as it is in heaven."'*

If we don't activate our human abilities and responsibilities in a kingdom call, we're going to miss out. In past decades when 're-vival' teaching was popular, we were given the impression that 'revival is coming – basically all we need to do is just wait for God to turn up, and do whatever He wants you to do. Then, when He comes, everything will be changed.'

That isn't really how the *Bible* sees it. The *Bible* says God has given you and me His word. We believe His word, we stand on the authority of His word and we walk with His word, and expect in faith to see Him move powerfully. Our Christianity is a partnership of God and us.

The church auditoriums we sit in today are here because someone gave money, time and expertise to build what God wanted. As a result, many lives have been impacted by God and a big part of the answer was the provision of finance that was required to build them.

One of the ministries that I have been involved in for many years, which I thank God for, is LIFETV, here in New Zealand. It is a contemporary TV program, through which multiple thousands of people have been ministered to and have found Christ. Without doubt, it is money that enables us to put the programs together, get air time etc. Again, without God we have nothing, but – unapologetically – it is money that allows the hungry to be fed and those without it to experience first-hand the tangible love of God. Never allow a resistance to money as an agent for the kingdom to enter your thinking. The enemy is continually seeking to keep the work of Christ weak through a lack of supply.

Please don't tell me that we don't need to focus on money, because, no matter where you are with your finances, God's purposes need more. Money says to a dream that is born out of the Spirit of God, we can create a vehicle to carry that. It is time for all of us to lift our commitment to see God's kingdom materialize.

**Ecclesiastes 10:18** *Because of laziness the building decays, and through idleness of hands the house leaks.*

## USING THE KEY IN YOUR HAND
In *Matthew 16:19*, Jesus tells Simon Peter He will give him: 'the keys of the kingdom of heaven, and whatever you bind on earth

will be bound in heaven, and whatever you loose on earth will be loosed in heaven.' We can have every key to open every lock, but until we activate the right key for the right door, the door remains fastened. That's why the Church can be filled with different kinds of people, sitting under similar teaching yet producing very different results and fruit in their lives. Whilst some are continuing to experience the breakthrough power of God, others, responding to the same word with an 'uh-huh' attitude, find little in their lives ever changes.

I don't know what it is that remains locked up in your world. Maybe it is a lack of personal freedom, or maybe it's dominant debt or an inability to create a financial platform for future generations. Jesus is going to build His Church based on our revelation of who He is. Seeing past our challenges, by fixing our eyes on who Jesus is and what He has promised to do, and then walking the right pathway will create all the difference.

If we do that, we're going to discover the keys of the kingdom and the truth that whatever we bind on earth will be bound in heaven. When we begin to understand what is bound and what is loosed in heaven, this should translate to our everyday lives. Then we will bind and we will loose the same here on earth.

I believe this passage in *Matthew* is literally asking, 'Why do you live bound to certain things when you have a right and authority to bind them? Why do you live with God's blessing not coming your way, when you have the capacity to be able to release it?'

I have never seen money turn up that does not have serial numbers on it. It was produced by a machine made by a human hand. If you were to receive a million dollars in cash with no serial numbers, it would be counterfeit and worth nothing. Yet we buy into the myth that God will change the world without a revelation of the release of money? The kingdom of heaven is built with both

## The kingdom of heaven is built with both spiritual and material things

spiritual and material things.

**1 Timothy 6:17-19** *Those who are rich in this present age [are] not to be haughty, nor to trust in uncertain riches but in the living God, who gives us richly all things to enjoy. Let them do good, that they be rich in good works, ready to give, willing to share, storing up for themselves a good foundation for the time to come, that they may lay hold on eternal life.*

We've established that money should never be our ruler and that His kingdom is released here on earth by our mastery over the way we use it. Even so, do we think of our money as entirely ours? Is it a private matter and our business what we do with it? This seems just the right moment to take a close look at how our theology is reflected in what our checkbooks reveal to us.

Myth Six takes a look at our discomfort around anyone else knowing what we do with our money. What's the biblical take on financial transparency?

# SIX

# CHECKBOOK THEOLOGY

───────────

How closely do you think your money and your faith are intertwined? Does how you spend your money have anything at all to say about your relationship with God?

As a pastor for more than 35 years, I've found it amazing how many times people have said to me, 'I'd get uncomfortable if people were to know what I do with my money.' Even though this may be a common feeling, it comes from a belief that our money is ours and that it is separate from our walk with God.

That's very different from how God sees it. As author Randy Alcorn notes in *The Treasure Principle*, 'Jesus spent more time teaching on money than on heaven and hell combined. Why? Because there's a fundamental connection between our spiritual lives and how we think about and handle money. We may try and divorce our faith and our finances, but God sees them as inseparable.'

Evangelist Billy Graham once said, 'You can tell where somebody's

> We may try and divorce our faith and our finances, but God sees them as inseparable

life is at by taking time to look at their checkbook.' Or, in today's terms, at their bank statements.

The enemy wants to distract us or dissolve our sense of responsibility when it comes to money. He works very hard at preventing us from reaching a place where we are completely open for God to bring kingdom blessing. Could you stand and have your money management revealed in full transparency before the courts of your King? If you subscribe to Myth Six, you might start to feel the pressure here.

## MYTH SIX – 'MY MONEY RESPONSE IS A PRIVATE AFFAIR'

People say, 'But doesn't the *Bible* say your right hand shouldn't know what your left hand is doing?' Let's go to the *Bible* and read about that.

*Matthew 6:1-4 Take heed that you do not do your charitable deeds before men, to be seen by them. Otherwise you have no reward from your Father in heaven. Therefore, when you do a charitable deed, do not sound a trumpet before you as the hypocrites do in the synagogues and in the streets, that they may have glory from men. Assuredly, I say to you, they have their reward. But when you do a charitable deed, do not let your left hand know what your right hand is doing, that your charitable deed may be in secret; and your Father who sees in secret will Himself reward you openly.*

If you stop and think about it, you will see that this scripture is all to do with motive. If we're giving so we receive the applause of men, Jesus says we are acting like the Pharisees. Their motive was impure. They just wanted to show everybody that they were doing the right thing externally, when the truth was they were empty white sepulchres devoid of God's spirit within them. That's not the way to do it. We give because it's right. And our Father who sees in secret will bring it out into the open. So, what is the connection between that and the privacy of our finances?

## MONEY IS OUR TESTING GROUND

When Maree and I arrived in New Zealand, we were confronted by something quite different from what we'd experienced in Australia in the area of leadership and resources. People within the Church were so sensitive on the topics of leadership and money. We realized that because of that pushback, many churches were going nowhere. Yes, people had a belief in God and attended church on Sundays, but there was such a lack of revelation knowledge in these two areas. Believe it or not, money is one of God's main testing grounds.

> **Money is one of God's main testing grounds**

*Luke 16:11 Therefore if you have not been faithful in the unrighteous mammon, who will commit to your trust the true riches?*

In other words, if you are not faithful in the material things you've been given, why would God entrust to you a ministry responsibility that has a bearing into eternity? I think this scripture suggests that money is our testing ground. If I really wanted to turn up the heat right now, I would say: if you want to do something for God, God says, 'Well, let's first check out the way you deal with money. I want to observe where your faith is when it comes to finance, where your trust is, where the priority of your security is, to determine whether or not you are ready to be entrusted with more.'

*1 Timothy 3:8* says that if you want to appoint a deacon in the church, one key qualification is that they must be wise with money. How do you know if they're wise with money? Because there's an openness about what's happening with their finances. I would say that in all areas of our lives, if we fail to have the right levels of accountability, we will experience limited breakthrough. Why would we hide what's happening with our money unless it has an authority over us that it shouldn't have? We will deal with that later in the book.

## HIDDEN BECOMES KNOWN

Let's go a step further. In *Mark 12:41-44*, Jesus is sitting in a church meeting, watching people give to the treasury. (Imagine the reaction if we did that today!) I like to try and picture the occasion in my mind's eye. When the offering is taking place, Jesus sits opposite where the money is being collected in big copper containers. He sees people who are rich, and people who are not so rich. And then He says to His disciples (my paraphrasing): 'It's an amazing thing. Many think they've given much, but they have just given little, as it has come out of their overflow.'

In other words, they gave out of their excess and in truth they barely noticed the impact. That was so unlike the poor widow, who, although she put in only a few coins, gave everything that she had. What was done in private was seen by all. It was all exposed.

I remember growing up in a church that passed around those velvet collection bags that hung down on a narrow wooden frame. I'm not sure whether the very small opening was intended to stop people from putting their hands in to steal money (or get change!) or so the person sitting next to you couldn't see how much you put in. I would suggest that, whether it's a touchy issue or not, when you have to keep your giving private, there's still an issue that God wants to untangle in you.

It's a myth that things pertaining to money should be hidden. Accountability is needed in all areas of our lives. Why? Because if we need growth in that area, we need to open our hearts in the right kind of healthy environments filled with the wisdom we need.

## It's a myth that things pertaining to money should be hidden

The final two of our Eight Money Myths may be the most commonly held of all. Most of us at one time or another have told ourselves that 'everything would be different if I had more money' – would it, really? – or have struggled with the feeling that our finances are so messed up we won't ever see improvement. Both of these ways of thinking leave us feeling like victims, reacting to our circumstances rather than taking the initiative over them. We challenge this mind-set next.

# SEVEN

# EVERY EXCUSE
# CHALLENGED

Maybe the most pervasive of all the wrong thinking about money is (Myth Seven) the idea that 'things would be different if I just had more money'. Another is when we find ourselves saying (Myth Eight), 'But I'm stuck and there's no way out'.

Even those of us who enjoy a comfortable income entertain 'What if' escapist scenarios of how life would change for the better if we had more money. Yet a recent *Reader's Digest* article reported that the 'big winners' in lotteries, whether they scored $6 million or $100 million, generally spent or lost all of it within five years. Research on windfall riches, carried out in a 2008 Dutch study, has shown that after the initial glow has faded, those who enjoyed big wins end up, within six months, no happier than they were before.

It reminds me of the story of a man who came to Peter Marshall, the Chaplain of the United States Senate in the late 1940s. He was concerned with tithing, and he said to Dr Marshall, 'I have a problem. I've been tithing for some time. It wasn't too bad when I started out working. I was making $20,000 a year and I could afford to give $2,000. But, you see, Peter, I'm now making $500,000 a year, and there's just no way that I can afford a tithe of $50,000.'

Dr Marshall reflected on the wealthy man's dilemma, but offered him no advice. He simply said, 'Yes, sir, I think you do have a problem. I think what we ought to do is pray right now. Would that be OK?' The man agreed. So Dr Marshall bowed his head, put his hand on the man's shoulder and prayed with boldness and authority: 'Dear Lord, this man has a problem. I pray that you help him, Lord. I pray that you reduce his salary back to the place where he can afford to tithe.'

You may laugh, but one of the big 'God tests' in your life if you are to fulfill God's purpose for your future is, 'What do I do with what I have right now?' And the very best place to start that examination is with Myth Seven – the idea that things would be different if we just had more money.

## MYTH SEVEN – 'IT WOULD BE DIFFERENT IF I HAD MORE'

Really? Scripture reminds us again and again of the divine law that there's a harvest in every seed.

After the flood, God promises Noah He will never flood the entire earth again and then gives this promise, which still stands today:

**Genesis 8:22** *While the earth remains, seedtime and harvest, cold and heat, winter and summer, and day and night shall not cease.*

Our answer is founded in the seed we possess today rather than the miracle we need tomorrow.

To believe we don't have enough is a way of thinking that we need to commit to dismantle. There can be so many excuses, 'If I had a better job… But if this changed… Or if that changed… If the kids didn't need braces… If my spouse worked longer hours…'

There's no better time than right now and no better place than right here to establish the fact that it is today's responses that determine tomorrow's outcomes. I hope you are beginning to believe in a far more prosperous future. It begins with God's help by confronting every myth that stands in our way.

> It is today's responses that determine tomorrow's outcomes

Every farmer believes in the authority of a sown seed to produce a harvest, and we, too, need to stop looking at our lack and start activating our current seed potential. Without doubt, the higher the mountain, the harder it is to climb; yet every mountain has a top that can be reached. We all have the power of harvest in our hand.

**MYTH EIGHT – 'I'M STUCK AND THERE'S NO WAY OUT'**
I think a vast percentage of the Church has this feeling that they can't escape because lack or debt has ruled for so long. Once again, we can't afford to allow the patterns of the past to determine the pathway into our future.

If you're stuck, like a fly in honey, it's my desire to pray and teach the 'stuckness' off you, to set you free to fly again. I've come to realize, because of God's word and the principles in this book, that it is never over when it comes to our much-needed financial victory. If there is an all-able God whose word is true, then there are divine principles that can release every one of us from financial barriers.

One of these key principles is found in the following passage.

*Deuteronomy 8:18 And you shall remember the Lord your God, for it is He who gives you power to get wealth, that He may establish His covenant which He swore to your fathers, as it is this day.*

This verse will echo through the rest of our teaching on this topic of *God Money & Me.* I strongly encourage you to get hold of this truth. God does not get wealth for you. Write it down and remind yourself. God empowers you to get wealth. If you are saying to yourself, 'I'm waiting for it to turn up in the mail', you shouldn't be making that many trips to your letterbox. It is time to get out of your armchair and begin to say,

---

## God empowers you to get wealth

---

'God, what is the pathway I've got to walk?' You might say, 'I don't know what the pathway is.' Again, my prayer is that through the revelation of God's word, the guidance of the Holy Spirit and the inspiration of this book, you will walk into a future of increasing financial release.

It is God who gives you the 'power to get wealth, that He may establish His covenant'. That means for all of us that we can be in a position to be able to fully have sufficiency in all things. Then add this to your arsenal:

*Jeremiah 17:7-8 Blessed is the man who trusts in the LORD, and whose hope is the LORD. For he shall be like a tree planted by the waters, which spreads out its roots by the river, and will not fear when heat comes; but its leaf will be green, and will not be anxious in the year of drought, nor will cease from yielding fruit.*

Are you already like 'a tree planted by the waters'? If not, then you might be saying, 'God, maybe I need to change some things. I've got to change the path I've been on, and go Your way. I'm going to have to trust and activate Your word.'

With that new trust comes a renewed expectation. For the one who trusts and hopes in the Lord 'shall be like a tree planted by the waters which spreads out its roots by the river'. It will not fear when the heat comes. Note that it doesn't promise that you won't go through hard times. But it does promise that your 'leaf will be green' and you 'will not be anxious in the year of drought'.

## GOD HASN'T FINISHED YET

You might say, 'I've been faithful to God, but, gosh, I'm in a drought season now.' Yes, we all go through drought seasons. But even in a drought we will not cease from producing fruit, because we understand God prepares us in the toughest of times for a stronger tomorrow.

God searches our hearts, tests our minds and examines our thinking to see whether we realize that we are blessed and that we are called to multiply and take dominion. He will give to us according to our ways, and according to the fruit of our actions.

That's a challenge. Between the promise and provision is the place of my responsibility. To trust is to walk with increasing expectation. It's all part of the biblical pattern that we will continue to define.

> Between the promise and provision is the place of my responsibility

If John Calvin's statement that 'where riches hold the dominion of the heart, God has lost His authority' has an ounce of truth, many of us are in big trouble. You can take it in two ways. You may be somebody who has nothing, deep in debt, which is dictating your level of hope and your ability to trust God's word. You feel under the control of your lack, and cannot see God's way through.

Or, on the other end of the scale, you may feel secure in your level of finances, and right now you find yourself allowing that security to distract you from the purposes of God for your life. What a sad thing it would be, to be in a place where God is wanting to do so much more but we are giving Him no opportunity to do so. When we don't handle money God's way, He has no authority in the financial areas of our lives.

Whatever state we find ourselves in, either negotiating lack or enjoying financial security, our human hearts are vulnerable. This world, our families, and the future generations need us to allow God to obtain access to our hearts in this crucial area.

Remember, you may feel stuck but you're not – there is a God way out. In Part Two of *God Money & Me*, we will start to unravel the shocking reality of how money gains a spirit the moment it touches a human hand, and we'll continue to establish a way to find financial freedom.

# MONEY MYTHS

---

Money often determines more of our life choices than we choose to acknowledge. Although it may be one of life's most powerful forces, we are all able to gain freedom from its control.

If John Calvin's statement 'Where riches hold the dominion of the heart, God has lost His authority' has an ounce of truth, many of us are in big trouble.

God has a plan for our financial freedom, clearly outlined in the *Bible*. Once embraced, we can create a pathway to financial freedom and a newfound liberty on every front. However, realigning our human responses to His purpose may require some reprogramming of our thinking.

Take a few quiet moments and ask the Holy Spirit this question: 'How can I allow God full and free access into my material world, so I can be fruitful and multiply?'

**MAIN REFLECTION POINTS:**

1. Financial breakthrough always seems to attract attention –
   Why do you think this is?

   _____

   _____

   _____

   _____

   _____

   _____

2. God  has blessed us and wants us to be fruitful, multiply and
   have dominion – What does this mean to you and has it been
   a focus in your finances?

   _____

   _____

   _____

   _____

   _____

   _____

3. Money either limits or liberates us – Explain more fully how
   you would see this.

   _____

   _____

   _____

   _____

   _____

   _____

4. What revelation and/or challenge is contained within *2 Corinthians 9:8* for where you are right now in your financial world?

5. If money weren't a limitation, how would you focus on changing the world? Name a couple of areas you would sow finances into.

6. Of the eight money myths mentioned, list the four that challenge you the most and explain why.

7. What is the biggest personal revelation you received from Part One of *God Money & Me*?

# PART TWO
# MONEY'S SPIRIT

# EIGHT

# MONEY – GOD'S TOOL OR THE ENEMY'S WEAPON

L ike me, I am sure that occasionally you've fallen victim to purchasing something and then, in hindsight, regretted the expense. It is so easy to fall into the trap of spending money you don't have, to buy things you don't want, to impress people you don't like'.

Actor Will Smith is often credited with coining this phrase, but actually its source dates back a lot further than him. Newspaper columnist Walter Winchell was quoted in the *Reader's Digest* in 1935 as saying: 'Broadway is a place where people spend money they haven't earned to buy things they don't need to impress people they don't like.' But the sentiment pre-dates Winchell, almost certainly going back to the early years of the

> Are you spending money you don't have, to buy things you don't want, to impress people you don't like?

twentieth century. So, the phenomenon of buying stuff you don't want to satisfy that drive for 'instant gratification' is not just a 'millennial' dilemma; it's been around long enough for us to conclude it's commonplace and a constant human temptation.

Often subtle and insiduous, but disastrous in effect, is when money allows mammon to attach, as mammon has an ultimate goal to rule and control. (This will be discussed in greater depth in later chapters.) If you find yourself habitually over-spending and therefore consequently living deeply in the red, you may be asking how you can break the power that debt holds over your life. I believe God has a plan for this, moving you from that place of feeling powerless when it comes to stewardship of finance to one of realizing God's promised blessing.

The truth is that we've drifted a long way from the design of God when it comes to handling our finances and often are unwise in making good practical decisions regarding it. It concerns me deeply that the modern Church seems to sit uncomfortably at opposite ends of the spectrum when teaching about money. Some churches are very focused and spend the majority of their time teaching about the need to give more, verging at times on manipulation, whilst others are reluctant to tackle the subject, evading full biblical counsel and practical instruction on how to create a financial future.

The *Bible* says that God is a liberating God. Jesus said that when we find truth, it sets us free *(John 8:32)*. In *Genesis 1*, we began by seeing that when God created Adam and Eve, He blessed them. Not just 'He blessed them for a time or a season'; no, 'He blessed them − full stop!' I don't know why it is that we stop believing that we can continually live in the blessing of God. This blessing is followed by a command: 'Now you be fruitful. Now you multiply. Now you take dominion' (paraphrased).

When you trust the God who made you, and as you step into His design and purposes, there is a way to unlock fruitfulness.

> As you step into His design and purposes, there is a way to unlock fruitfulness

You – and your resources – have the power to expand. Instead of being dominated by something that desires to shrink and reduce you, make a decision to arrest and take control over it.

You can take confidence that God your Father is good, trust that Jesus has made a complete way for you to know Him and understand that every promise He has given belongs to you as one of His children. It is time to understand what it is in our lives that is limiting the purposes of God, particularly when it comes to money.

### KING DAVID'S LESSON

As I read the *Bible*, I try to gain some insight into the spirit of the people whose lives are included in it. When I read a verse, I often personalize it by asking the Holy Spirit, 'What are You trying to say to me?' In the Old Testament, before crowning Solomon as next in line, King David commissioned his son and the people of his day with the honor of building the temple for God. David's love for God was evident when he challenged Israel with the question: 'Why is it that we spend money on ourselves and our homes while the house of God lies in ruin?'

King David stirs them and encourages their hearts by saying, 'Let's do something together for God'. I love the prayer he leads the people in as they bring their offerings;

*1 Chronicles 29:12 Both riches and honor come from You, and You reign over all.*

Maybe for some of us this is a needed revelation. God doesn't remove Himself from the equation when 'riches' are mentioned. No: 'Both riches and honor come from You, and You reign over all.'

Even if we don't feel comfortable discussing it, money – along with many other things – is a crucial subject. It's funny to note that when Maree and I have taught on relational issues, and spoken to churches about marriage, often sex is a subject that we address as it needs to be talked about. Some people comment, 'Should you talk that candidly about sex in a church environment?' Well, God made sex. God doesn't go, 'Sex? Ooh!' Seriously! Just because the world's tainted it, it doesn't mean we should accept that spoiled picture and avoid any discussion. So it is with finance; with God's blessing, it can build and bring much-needed change while creating a pathway for the gospel.

> God doesn't remove Himself from the equation when 'riches' are mentioned

*1 Chronicles 29:12 You reign over all. In Your hand is power and might; in Your hand it is to make great and to give strength to all.*

Ezra declared that not only did God reign over all riches but God's hand was also able to make all things He ruled over great, mighty and infused with strength. God is invested and interested in all that He governs, our lives and our wealth included.

Again, *Proverbs 11* reminds us that we consistently have to challenge any thinking that limits our ability to be resourceful people who are empowered to bring blessing to our communities.

*Proverbs 11:10–11 When it goes well with the righteous, the city rejoices; and when the wicked perish, there is jubilation. By the blessing of the upright the city is exalted, but it is overthrown by the mouth of the wicked.*

When we get in tune with God on matters of money, breakthrough results and even the environment around us begins to change. However, there is a challenge: 'But it is overthrown by the mouth of the wicked.'

---

## Words can produce destruction or they can bring liberty

I believe it is easy to under-estimate the creative power of our words. Do you know words can produce destruction or they can bring liberty? Naturally the enemy doesn't want us to be talking about money and God's plan for us in it, because he wants to maintain control over what are the keys to releasing blessing. He wants us to say, 'It will never happen for me; I'll never get a breakthrough in my financial world; blessing is not part of my salvation.'

## THE GOOD MAN

**Psalm 37:23-24** *The steps of a good man are ordered by the Lord, and He delights in his way. Though he fall, he shall not be utterly cast down; for the Lord upholds him with His hand.*

Who is a 'good' man? We're not considered to be good because there is something inherently pure and righteous about us: we're good simply because we embrace the goodness of God. Once we choose to live God's way, our steps and thinking begin to align with the nature and practices of God, and the logical flow on from this is that our outcomes will be ordered by the Lord. God begins to step in and fashion a new pathway for us to walk on.

The reality is, we never get it all right and we will fall sometimes, but, as the psalmist says, though we fall, we're not cast down because God's hand lifts us up. I love how the psalmist continues:

***Psalm 37:25-26*** *I have been young, and now am old; yet I have not seen the righteous forsaken, nor his descendants begging bread. He is ever merciful, and lends; and his descendants are blessed.*

These are not my words. They are penned by the psalmist and inspired by the Spirit of God. 'Yet I have not seen the righteous forsaken.' To be righteous is not about being perfect or simply turning up to church. It is never about an outward appearance but rather an internal faith response to the grace of God and outworked by following His ways. Like many, I've spent a lot of my life facing the challenge of lack, and even though I knew God was good, I never fully understood how His kingdom worked in the realm of finance. The change began when I decided to face the myths I had believed about money.

## The change began when I decided to face the myths I had believed about money

What I've learned is that God isn't reluctant to bless us, and it is not money that is the problem; it's what money attracts as an attachment. We'll explain all about that 'spirit of mammon' in the next chapter.

# NINE

# THE SPIRIT OF MAMMON

In the previous chapter, we introduced the idea that it isn't money itself that is the problem, it's what attaches to it. The hopes, the dreams and often the reliance we put on money as the answer to all our problems very quickly become the problem itself. There's a term that's been used for centuries to describe what I'm talking about here, and that is the 'spirit of mammon'. Mammon is money that operates outside of the purposes of God, comparable to a 'money god'. According to scripture, it's a spirit that attaches itself to money if we fail to surrender it firstly to God.

> Mammon is. . . a spirit that attaches itself to money and operates outside the purposes of God

Even though we may have a belief in God, if we do not pursue an understanding of His kingdom ways, we often unwittingly give the enemy dominion over certain areas of our lives. Jesus taught that it is impossible to worship both God and money.

Once money has been given the power to direct our decisions, it has the authority to determine who we end up serving, and the consequence of that is both frightening and sobering.

The first recorded sin in the early Church was to do with the deception and control of money. Ananias and Sapphira sold a field and like many of the other first-century believers, we are told they brought the proceeds to the apostles to distribute to those in need. However, there was a significant flaw in their integrity: they wanted to enjoy the 'big show' of public giving – it had become the thing to do – but they had secretly kept back some of the proceeds for themselves. Although that was not a problem in itself, they lied about the fact that they had done so.

The dreadful consequence was they dropped dead within hours of each other. As the pre-eminent devotional *Bible* commentator Matthew Henry concluded: 'They thought they might serve both God and mammon. […] The crime of Ananias was not his retaining part of the price of the land; he might have kept it all, had he pleased; but his endeavouring to impose upon the apostles with an awful lie, from a desire to make a vain show […] if we think to put a cheat upon God, we shall put a fatal cheat upon our own souls.'

## MONEY IS A DIVINE TESTING GROUND

A similar deadly fate awaited Judas, as we are told he stole from the communal purse:

**John 12:6** *He was a thief; as keeper of the money bag, he used to help himself to what was put into it.* (NIV)

He betrayed Jesus for 30 pieces of silver and became riddled with regret almost immediately after the deed was done *(Matthew 26:15, Matthew 27:3)*. It really wasn't about the money, though: it was about mammon and the spirit behind what was done, and ultimately in both of these tragic scenarios it was the enemy's plan through mammon that took them out.

*Luke 16:10-11 He who is faithful in what is least is faithful also in much; and he who is unjust in what is least is unjust also in much. Therefore if you have not been faithful in the unrighteous mammon, who will commit to your trust the true riches?*

*Luke* teaches us that if we're faithful today, even though it seems small and inconsequential, tomorrow we will be entrusted to be faithful with much. If we are unjust – if we deal with today in a compromised way – then we will live a compromised tomorrow.

It's not ambiguous – God's word makes it clear: 'If you have not been faithful in the unrighteous mammon, who will commit to your trust the true riches?'

God is literally saying to us that money is a divine testing ground. Money, which is just a commodity of this world, is a test that God uses to determine what eternal things we are ready for. For me, this is such an important revelation and why every-thing around money seems to create such contention. Why wouldn't it, when the enemy knows that if we get the issues and understanding around money sorted, we will see so much more of God's kingdom here on earth?

## Money is a divine testing ground

## UNSURRENDERED MONEY

My definition of mammon would be 'unsurrendered money that is empowered to draw us away'. Because money and its accompanying divine assignment is ultimately owned by an all-able, all-providing, all-blessing God called El Shaddai, we must draw the conclusion that money's not the problem. However, once it reaches a human hand, one of two spirits will seek to attach its influence to it: the spirit of mammon or the spirit of El Shaddai.

---

**Mammon is unsurrendered money that is empowered to draw us away**

---

Four times in the *Bible* Jesus addresses the subject of mammon. We don't think about it very much because the enemy wants to keep it hidden, but another definition of mammon means 'confidence placed in riches'. Jesus calls it an evil spirit. In fact, it's the only evil spirit He ever names.

The gospels contain more warnings about the misuse of money than about any other subject. Could that be because the enemy is, for many of us, already using it to limit or distract the purposes of God through our lives? If that's the case, don't we need to bring this subject out into the light? Almost half the parables Jesus told made reference to money, and He said we need to be on guard even against coveting the things pertaining to money.

*Luke 16:12 And if you have not been faithful in what is another man's, who will give you what is your own?*

If you're a parent, think about that. If our children prove to be trustworthy in what we entrust to them, we feel confident that they are ready for more; but if they're not dependable with what they are given, we question their readiness. God works in the same way.

*Luke 16:13 No servant can serve two masters.*

No one can serve two masters at the same time. 'You will love one and hate the other, or be loyal to one and despise the other. You CANNOT serve God and mammon' (paraphrased, emphasis added).

You see, the enemy seeks to divide loyalties and he uses money to do so. All of us become a servant of whatever we give priority to. All of our beliefs and convictions in our Christian walk can flourish or be thwarted by what we prioritize.

## The enemy seeks to divide loyalties

If I were to pull out a $100 note from my pocket when walking down a busy street and began offering it to those who passed me by, I am sure, after a little hesitation, there would be a number of people prepared to take it from me. The reason is, money has an ability to feed and provide for us all in some way – which, of course, makes it desirable. The reality, however, – if you think about it – is that in most countries it is just a piece of colored paper, with an attached value.

In the same way, money itself has no morals attached to it whatsoever. It isn't bad or good, right or wrong. Yet, as soon as it touches the human hand, it attracts an attachment. If we respond to God's way with it, it has God's blessing/spirit all over it; if not, it becomes mammon, which will work at distracting us from the purposes of God.

When this became a revelation to me, I began to discover the importance of money and how I dealt with it the moment it came my way. Remember, money is the test for things that are of eternal significance.

Mammon has some cunning and sneaky ways to gain control

## Money is the test for things that are of eternal significance

in our thinking, which we will begin to examine in the next chapter. I want to suggest that not all 'golden' opportunities are 'God' opportunities. You know the old adage about business propositions – that if they sound too good to be true, they probably are? The same applies to some of the circumstances that seem to offer promotion, better money, or some real advance in your career or earning capacity.

I've seen many a good Christian man or woman 'sidelined' in their faith walk because they too readily chased after what looked like a fantastic new opportunity without examining closely enough whether or not it was in God's plan and purpose for them. For some the potential for making money became the basis of their decision and mammon once again became empowered to activate its authority.

> Ultimate financial freedom begins at the point where God has full authority in our material world

In the next chapter, I will explain how mammon's number-one form of attack is deception – and sometimes the offer looks so very attractive we think it must be right. Let's wise up to the enemy's tactic of deception, never allowing money to take the place of God. Ultimate financial freedom begins at the point where God has full authority in our material world.

# TEN

# MAMMON'S DEVICE IS DECEPTION

I'm not sure those first-century believers Ananias and Sapphira – introduced in the previous chapter – had any idea of how seriously they had drifted from God's true values when they decided to keep a little bit back from the sale price of their land and lie about it. The problem wasn't with the money they kept: it was the deception that came with their decision to lie once mammon had attached itself.

It's just as true today that we can easily deceive ourselves about our true intentions and values when it comes to God, money and us. We can be guilty of telling ourselves that we're managing our finances with integrity when, in fact, we can be operating far from the truth of God's word. To establish financial freedom and create a pathway for God's blessing, we are all to live according to the wisdom of the biblical patterns that He has ordained.

To illustrate my point, let me recount an experience I had with a couple I bumped into at a local store; they used to come to LIFE but I hadn't seen them for quite a while. I greeted them, 'Hi, guys, how are you going?' I could tell they were uncomfortable meeting up with me so unexpectedly. It was like, 'Ooh, it's the pastor.' Straightaway they began to apologize for not being in church for months, 'but you've got to understand how busy we are'. Before I could even open my mouth, they continued: 'Work is over the top; we're working five, six days a week. But we feel bad we haven't been in church.' I said, 'It's OK. You don't have to be accountable to me, but just make sure God gets first place, because He then can help you in everything you're going through.'

No doubt they were in a busy season, as the husband traveled into the city, where the church was located, from Monday to Friday, negotiating hectic traffic, and at times was also doing overtime on Saturday. So when it got to Sunday, he and his wife said to themselves, 'We're exhausted! We're just too tired.'

What's my point? It is that we'll drive ourselves to make some extra money even at the expense of being in God's house. You might say, 'So do we have to be in church?' No, you don't have to do anything you don't want to, but if that is God's plan, then His way works.

***Psalm 92:13-14*** *Those who are planted in the house of the* LORD *shall flourish in the courts of our God. They shall still bear fruit in old age; they shall be fresh and flourishing…*

Mammon seeks to get you to spend your whole week and ultimately your whole life pursuing money. Without you even being aware, it will seek to distract, and before you know it, your allegiance has been swayed and your priority has become money and not the

> Mammon seeks to get you to spend your whole week and ultimately your whole life pursuing money

kingdom of God. Let's take a look at the first of three key ways mammon operates to exert power and control over our lives.

## MAMMON'S DECEPTION IS CONTROL

Since satan is the father of lies, then naturally a major weapon in his arsenal is deception. Remember our discussion on *Luke 16:11*, where we are told: 'If you have not been faithful in the unrighteous mammon, who will commit to your trust the true riches?'

At the risk of repeating myself, I want to emphasize again – you are blessed and there is a significant purpose assigned to your life. There is a pathway for you to walk that produces fruitfulness, creates multiplication and requires dominion. Breakthrough into our full financial potential will ultimately leave a legacy for the generations that follow.

In the process of 'believing to the receiving' of all Jesus has promised, don't let the enemy confuse you if you are experiencing lack, as I was. I had to come to realize that no one is immune to the deception of mammon, but, despite this, the test is to choose to be faithful and resist living under the lying regime of our adversary.

> No one is immune to the deception of mammon

When we're deceived in any area, we don't know we're deceived. We may earnestly believe we have a relationship with God, that we're called to be in His house and to participate in building His kingdom. And then, as with the couple I mentioned at the start of this chapter, we devote all of our time to earning and serving money. We can often fall into the trap of saying to ourselves, 'Yeah, well, when I can tick off this goal and fulfill that obligation, then I'll genuinely start to serve you, God.' Really?

Let me be clear – there's absolutely nothing wrong with work and making money, but, according to Jesus, we can't serve two masters. It's actually irresponsible not to work hard; in fact, it is a fundamental key to seeing a financial breakthrough and moving from lack to more. Where it goes amiss and we find mammon taking charge is when the priority shifts and our focus becomes all about the money to the detriment of the purposes of God. No one is immune from allowing their heart to become caught up in wrong allegiances; however, the question has to continually be asked, 'What or whom am I serving?'

## WIRED FOR PROVISION

My experience over many years of observing a lot of believers is that there's a very low percentage of God's children who are ready to handle a lot of wealth and not succumb to the deception of that abundance. Money can achieve so much good and yet if we continue with limited understanding, partnered with unwise decisions, money will create an unhealthy outcome.

A great friend of mine, the late Pastor Sy Rogers, told me that when it comes to counseling in the Christian community, two of the main areas of concern are finance and sexual integrity. Basically, we were wired by God to do life together, while living within the boundaries of His word, to experience His provision.

Again and again Jesus taught the disciples to keep Him as the center of their devotion and identity. When our security becomes based on material things, we drift into the dangerous waters of deception.

Obviously, we require provision for everything we need today. God wants our lives to experience blessing and overflow, creating an answer for many in need.

The enemy understands how we are wired as well, and so uses mammon to promise the same outcomes. The deception is that mammon uses money and material things to become the source of what we need to secure fulfillment, happiness and worth. We can all so easily fall into the trap of placing our security in the bank rather than in God. Understanding the nature of deceit, we must always seek clarification in our heart as to whom we are serving – God or mammon?

Mammon whispers at times, 'Work a little harder, make your job and your income paramount, keep it of supreme importance, and people will begin to see you as successful and valued.' Before we know it, we're on that cyclic treadmill – we 'need' more and more, then to maintain what we've achieved, we have to keep 'doing' more and more.' What a trap!

## THE ENEMY'S GAME PLAN

God doesn't live in the shadows: He works out in the open and in the light, but the enemy is always operating behind a smokescreen. The enemy's not going to come out and expose the end result of serving mammon; instead, he hides in the shadows and seeks to mix a little truth with a lot of lies in his cocktail of deception. That's his game plan.

> The enemy ... seeks to mix a little truth with a lot of lies in his cocktail of deception

God, however, comes out in the open and clearly declares, 'I'm El Shaddai. I want to bless you and this is the pathway of blessings. No deception. Your choice. If you don't attach to Me, you will end up serving mammon.' Remember:

*Matthew 6:21 For where your treasure is, there your heart will be also.*

We often stop at this verse; yet in *Matthew 6:23* Jesus continues: 'But if your eye is bad, your whole body will be full of darkness.

If therefore the light that is in you is darkness, how great is that darkness!' In essence, Jesus is warning us that if we think we can compromise His lordship over our material world and stay in control, we are simply deluded.

Make no mistake, if mammon is in control and your life doesn't align with God's pathway, deception will take root and cause you to end up in a very dark place. You may be saying, 'But my financial world is in a dark place right now.' This is the very reason why I have written *God Money & Me* – to enable understanding of what to do next. Remember we are only in Part Two.

Our financial and material world operates either in a surrendered or unsurrendered position. If it is unsurrendered, it has the power to draw us away. Mammon begins with deception, but it does not stop there. It has a second agenda it is working toward, which is worship. That's what we'll explain in our next chapter in examining the ways mammon pulls us into its vortex.

> Our financial and material world operates either in a surrendered or unsurrendered position

# ELEVEN

# MAMMON'S GOAL IS WORSHIP

I faced a key test as a young man when I felt God call me to Sydney at the age of 20, and yet it was only years later that the full implications of my choice really came home to me. I'd left New Zealand, where I had grown up, with a clear sense that God wanted me to go and support a church my senior pastor had started. I arrived with not much more than a feeling that this was something God wanted me to do. I had been in Sydney for six months, and just couldn't find a job. Even though many people were generous towards me, I'd fallen into a financial hole. I believed that God had taken me there from New Zealand to help build the Church and yet I needed money to live.

God had called me to serve the Church, but at the time there were no staff positions. It seemed like every outside job I went for, the door closed. Long story short, after a considerable time, I finally got an interview – I'd had many that had fallen through, but this one was amazing. The base retainer was better than the salary I wanted. There was a promise of incredible commissions that would come through sales. The boss liked me, I liked him, and it was like, 'God, you've answered my prayers. You took a long time coming, but You've finally come through.'

I took the job, which seemed an answer to all my lack, and as I left the interview room, I was on such a high. I had just got through the door when the interviewer called out to me: 'By the way, our two busiest days are Saturday and Sunday.' I said, 'What do you mean, every weekend?' He said, 'Yeah, every weekend.' I hesitated, knowing I had come to help build God's house, but found myself responding, 'OK, that's fine, I'll take it.'

Excited and yet confused, I went to where my car was parked, turned the ignition on and headed home. I will never forget what happened next. Have you ever been in a situation where you feel the Holy Spirit sitting right next to you and He is looking straight at you? I knew I was about to be challenged by the decision I had just made, so I decided I wasn't going to look His way. My deflection mechanism was to turn the music up. Gently and yet consistently, I felt the Holy Spirit saying, 'So you'd take that job, huh?' I knew the Holy Spirit was asking me against all odds to trust Him and put God first. By the end of that miserable drive, I knew what I had to do. When I got home, I rang that boss and tried to explain. Just 20 minutes beforehand, I'd been telling him how much of a miracle this job offer was and how much I needed it. Now, I said, 'Sir, I'm sorry. You might never understand this, but I can't take that job if I have to work on a Sunday.'

Now I'm not saying for a moment that to work on a Sunday is wrong. But, for me, I knew what God had asked me to do. To worship God is to position Him first. I wonder at times if I'd be doing what I am doing today if I had not made that choice. Mammon toils relentlessly for our loyalty in order to secure our worship.

It's important that we recognize that not all the opportunities that appear as though they are there to bless us may be right for us. I remember a couple we were offering pastoral care to as they had deep issues and had been struggling in their relationship for quite a long time. They made a decision that I believe the enemy used to destroy their last seeds of hope.

> **Mammon toils relentlessly for our loyalty in order to secure our worship**

In the middle of the season of marriage counsel, the husband received a job offer in another city promising greater financial reward. He accepted the offer and he and his wife moved without any further communication. The outcome became that they couldn't find a church family they were comfortable with, their attendance dwindled, and finally they separated and their marriage was over. When money becomes the priority component in our decisions, we may not understand but we have begun to worship it. It's so important that we don't allow deception to lead us to worship the wrong things. Remember, mammon's goal is worship.

We must never forget that satan fell as one of the angels in heaven because he saw himself as the one to be worshiped. His agenda hasn't changed – he still wants to be worshiped today. But he is not foolish enough to come out blatantly and cry, 'Bow down, worship me!' No, he's much more subtle. Once he has you chasing after money as your ultimate prize, he'll have started the journey of claiming rule in your heart and from there he will have your worship.

## TRUE FOUNDATIONS REVEALED

In *Matthew 4:1-11*, we are given the account of Jesus as He was preparing for ministry. The Spirit had led Him into the wilderness to be tempted by the devil. He's been fasting for 40 days when satan comes and says, 'You're hungry.' Jesus goes, 'Yeah.' The devil says, 'You can command these stones to become bread.' That's an enticing option. To be honest, after even one day of fasting, I'd find that tempting. But Jesus says, 'No, there's something going on here. Man shall not live by bread alone, but by every word that proceeds from the mouth of God.' This was the first test Jesus faced – **The Test of Provision.**

Next, the devil takes Jesus to the pinnacle of the temple and says, 'You're the Son of God. Throw Yourself down, and angels will come from all eternity.' He has no doubts about angelic existence since he used to be one. He even had the audacity to promise on behalf of the divine guardians that Jesus would 'not dash His foot against a stone'. What does Christ do? He responds, 'I'm not here to prove My value to you. You shall not tempt the Lord your God.' That's the second test – **The Test of Security.**

Finally, the devil takes Jesus to an exceedingly high mountain and shows Him all the kingdoms of the world in their glory. And he says to Him, 'All these things I will give You if You fall down and worship me.' And that's the third test – **The Test of Lordship.**

Every one of us has an enemy coming at us in the same way. To be honest, the concept of worshiping money may seem far-fetched. But if money is our priority, and our ultimate decision-maker, if it takes the things of God and puts them second, it's the object of our worship.

> If money is our priority and decision-maker . . . it's the object of our worship

Jesus said to satan, 'It is written, "You shall worship the LORD your God"' – no excuses – '"and Him only you shall serve."' And I believe He would say the same to us.

A rich young ruler came to Jesus and said, 'I have an abundance of wealth, but what must I do to have You?' Jesus said, 'For you, unfortunately, it's not just that you've got money, it's that money's got you. You believe in Me and have kept many of My commandments but your test will be to sell everything you have' (*Matthew 19:16-22*, paraphrased). The ruler left full of sorrow, because, for him, money had become his god.

Never allow your major decisions over jobs and futures ever take precedence over what God's asking you to do or have. Stay alert to the deceptive devices of mammon, who seeks to secure your worship.

Can you see the progression employed by the spirit of mammon to imprison you? If mammon deceives us into worship, ultimately we will be under its control. That's what we will examine in this final section – how to avoid getting under mammon's control.

# TWELVE

# MAMMON'S OUTCOME IS CONTROL

I will never forget when Maree and I went with a few other couples on our first-ever cruise, to celebrate 25 years of marriage. It was an amazing experience to be part of a crowd of 4,000-plus passengers. The food was simply top shelf, and we spent seven days eating, going to the gym and stopping at ports in countries we had never been to before. We had so much fun and it was an amazing holiday.

While we were in the middle of our cruise, the Global Financial Crisis hit. What took place around us when the news of the crash came on TV was simply unreal. The warm, fun-filled atmosphere – people playing in the pool, relaxing, having massages – completely changed. Instead, people everywhere were crowded in front of TV screens listening for how bad the stock-market fall had been. People were on their phones to their stockbrokers and confusion and pain were visible everywhere. Joy and fun had turned into fear and deep-seated apprehension. You could see on so many faces the devastation of it all.

You have to ask the question – Why? For many, their futures and trust were completely centered on financial security and possessions. Mammon had clearly taken the driver's seat. But, when you have taken its bait – which is so easy for any of us to do – and offered the security of your life to wealth and belongings, then the 'fear of loss' becomes a cruel taskmaster. This reinforces what we read in *Luke*:

**Luke 16:13** *No one can serve two masters. Either you will hate the one and love the other, or you will be devoted to the one and despise the other.* (NIV)

## MAMMON DIVIDES OUR LOYALTIES

**Luke 16:10** *He who is faithful in what is least is faithful also in much; and he who is unjust in what is least is unjust also in much.*

Not one of us can be loyal to mammon and also be loyal to God. Or, to turn it around: we can't put God first and at the same time base our security on possessions. We cannot have two masters. If we don't surrender money and material things to El Shaddai, then our money and material world will ultimately overpower us and we will be drawn towards mammon's authority. Sooner or later, we're controlled by the very thing that we thought would be a blessing to ourselves and others. Fundamentally this comes down to the issue of lordship.

> We can't put God first and also base our security on possessions

**Isaiah 26:3** *You will keep him in perfect peace whose mind is stayed on you.*

Whenever money becomes something we contemplate more than we think about God, our priorities have already begun to shift. God doesn't 'beat around the bush'. He says that every time money comes to us, it has the potential of going two ways. If we trust Him with it, He'll keep us from the deception, the worship and the control of mammon. Take a moment to ponder the following verses.

---

**Every time money comes to us, it has the potential of going two ways**

---

*Jeremiah 17:7-8 Blessed is the man who trusts in the LORD, and whose hope is the LORD. For he shall be like a tree planted by the waters, which spreads out its roots by the river, and will not fear when heat comes; but its leaf will be green, and will not be anxious in the year of drought, nor will cease from yielding fruit.*

Blessed, happy, fortunate, to be envied is the one whose priority is in the Lord.

The basis of a blessed financial future is founded within the nature of God to bless us. God creates a pathway in every wilderness and has a plan for what He has promised in every single area of our lives. Wherever we find ourselves today, God has the answer. The curse of mammon will lose its control once we understand how mammon works and decide to live according to God's plan for our future.

In *Jeremiah*, God tells us that we 'shall be like a tree that is planted by the waters. It spreads out its roots by the river. It does not fear when heat comes' (paraphrased). Notice that God makes it clear we will have seasons of heat but He has an answer to every challenge.

## THE PRINCIPLE OF THE FIRST
Let me put it out there: I don't believe God wants us to live limited in any respect. The challenge has always been, and remains today, to understand that our response to God's word determines the

shape of our future. Imagine for a moment how effective we could be in serving God if we were financially free.

In that passage of *Jeremiah* we were just considering, the challenge is issued and the heat is really applied when God says, 'I, the Lord, search your heart' (paraphrased).

**Jeremiah 17:10** *I, the LORD, search the heart, I test the mind, even to give every man according to his ways, according to the fruit of his doings.*

God always looks at heart motive. He searches our innermost thoughts. The moment we align our heart, everything else changes. Everything long term stems from a heart issue. Life tells us that. If we've got bad roots, we'll produce bad fruit, and, conversely, the opposite is also true.

God is saying (my paraphrasing): 'I search the heart and search the mind – the thinking – to give to every man according to his ways, according to the fruit of his doings.' The right spirit mixed with the right responses is the base plate for so much more.

> The right spirit mixed with the right responses is the base plate for so much more

We have established that when money comes into our lives – whether we receive it, inherit it or earn it –, it gains a spirit as soon as it touches our hands. If we've got the right heart, and honor God with it, deflecting all the lies and the false promises the enemy has sent our way, then we're going to release a God-enlarged future.

## FIRST RELEASES THE REST

There is an important principle at work here. I call it the 'first releases the rest' principle. This comes into effect whether you have little – when you feel like you are only just scraping through every week – or you have plenty. If God is first in your increase you will see His blessing.

How do we guard against mammon ever being the source of our security and the thing we end up worshiping? Remember what John Calvin said: 'Where riches hold the dominion of your heart, God has lost His authority.'

God has given each one of us the power of choice. You could say, 'Well, I just don't want to put God first.' You have that choice. No one has the right to make you do anything. Not even God will make you do what brings financial release. But if you choose to live in obedience, you release the power of El Shaddai over your material world.

## Money attracts a spirit to it

One more time: Money attracts a spirit to it. It's either mammon or it's the blessing of a limitless and all-able God. Challenging, eh?

I encourage you to make a statement over your life today: 'God, I am putting Your spirit over what's coming my way, and over what I already have.'

That's how you break the dominion that mammon seeks. Everything we own is really not ours: it has been entrusted ultimately for a greater kingdom purpose. Yes, we are to enjoy it – there's nothing wrong with that. However, if you've never put God first in your finances, you are yet to experience what happens when God gets involved.

If we get this correct, we are well under way to seeing our children and our children's children blessed because of our obedience. They can be positioned materially to be making their decisions based on what God wants them to do, not money. In Part One and Part Two we have laid a foundation to what is about to come. In Part Three, Money's Test, we will examine how to ensure God remains sovereign over our increase.

# MONEY SPIRIT

---

Once our focus and primary answer to life becomes more money, we easily fall under the spell of mammon. Mammon is 'unsurrendered money that has the power to draw us away.' God wants to bless us, but how we respond to what we receive determines our future. Remember: it is not money that is the problem, but what spirit attaches itself to it.

God uses money and wants to create a financial future but this is determined by who or what has the position of authority. Every one of us has been given the opportunity to choose so we can release God's authority in and over our financial world.

## MAIN REFLECTION POINTS:

1. Write out *Proverbs 11:10-11*. Explain what this means to you.

2. Why do you think God has chosen money as a testing ground?
   *Luke 16:10-11*

3. Explain how mammon gains a right to attach itself to our
   material world and ultimately us.

4. How does mammon deceive us? Give an example from your life of how this has happened in your past.

5. What is mammon's ultimate goal and why?

6. What is the biggest personal revelation for you from Part Two of *God Money & Me*?

7. Write out your own definition of mammon.

# PART THREE
# MONEY'S TEST

# THIRTEEN

# THE FOUNDATION FOR FINANCIAL FREEDOM

———

Like many, you may have privately asked yourself: 'Why is there so much suffering through poverty in this world when God is a God of love?'

We may well hear God respond, reminding us, as followers of God, that our mandate is missional in bringing solutions to a needy world. Our challenge, therefore, is ensuring our personal financial situation doesn't thwart our ability to assist the needs of others.

Unfortunately, when it comes to God's financial wisdom and economy, we often only hear messages in the church that focus more on the 'giving out' – to the detriment of being taught how to build a greater financial base so we can become more of an answer to need long term. We may have missed the wider view, the bigger picture. It is my desire in the forthcoming chapters of this book to bring you a fuller perspective. I do, however, want to begin at the foundational truth on which we build our financial future and it involves the tithe. Contrary to much spiritual teaching, tithing isn't the only ingredient required for personal financial breakthrough, but it is an unquestionable start.

The groundwork for building financial freedom begins with a clear understanding about tithing – it is simply ensuring that the first 10 percent of all of our increase is returned to God. For some, this statement could make you feel decidedly uncomfortable. I fully understand, but encourage you to stay open and keep reading all the way to the end of the book. I believe you will discover a fuller comprehensive view of the way God works when it comes to ensuring mammon has no way of access into our material world.

Often our hesitation to embrace the principle of tithing is because there has been much debate and lack of clarity about this topic. It's frowned on and criticized by those outside the Church as some antiquated rule designed to limit, rob and control people and line the pockets of a few leaders. It has at times also been resented by many within the house of God, possibly for some of the same reasons. I suppose this shouldn't take us by surprise; as we have already discovered, mammon is at work and the enemy knows what happens when we put God first in this area.

## THE CHALLENGE AND THE SOLUTION

*Relevant* magazine published an interesting report, *What Would Happen If The Church Tithed* – released in 2013 and again in March 2016 – that investigated the worldwide Church and came to this conclusion: somewhere between 10 and 25 percent of the Church tithe consistently. So, that means approximately eight out of ten 'born-again, believing' Christians don't tithe consistently. Here is the bottom line, whether we like it or not: if we fail to return to God what belongs to Him, He will not have sovereignty and authority over our financial world; mammon will.

In light of those previous statistics, we can assume one in five of those who profess to be believing Christians live under an open

> If we fail to return to God what belongs to Him, He will not have sovereignty and authority over our financial world; mammon will

heaven with regards to God's provision and protection in material things. That's when you realize how crucial this issue really is. The study found that Christians are giving 2.5 percent of their gross income per capita. Yet when they went back and looked at statistics from the Great Depression, Christians were then giving 3.3 percent. It seems the more we receive, the less likely we are to honor God in this way.

You may question: 'Well, Paul, I'm not sure tithing is for today', or may feel 'I am simply unable to tithe as I just don't have much.' We will dig deeper to gain a clearer understanding on both these issues further into the book. Here's a thought, though: did you know that one billion people live on less than a $1 a day? It does bring a little perspective to our own finances at times when we feel like we are struggling to have enough.

The above-mentioned study also showed that if the Church were to tithe fully, there would be an extra $165 billion per year available for what God wants to do to fulfill His purposes here on earth. With that amount of extraordinary resource maybe we could become so much more of a means to answer the needs that surround us. That's not $165 million: that's $165 billion. These are mind-boggling figures. Just imagine. . .

If all Christians who say they put God first actually followed His prescription for material breakthrough and tithed as the first key, the global impact would be phenomenal. Take a look below.

It was calculated that:
- $25 billion every year could relieve global hunger, starvation

and deaths from preventable diseases in just 5 years;
- $12 billion could eliminate illiteracy in 5 years;
- $15 billion could solve all of the world's water and sanitary problems, specifically in areas where people live on less than $1 a day; and
- $1 billion could fully fund all overseas missions' work.

And, every year, there would still remain an excess of between $100 billion and $110 billion that could be used to propagate the purposes of God.

Imagine the difference the Church could make if we would just do things God's way. And yet people say, 'Well I don't believe in tithing, that's Old Testament.' My response is that it's absolutely in the Old Testament, but to draw the conclusion that tithing is only an Old Testament law is a flawed theology.

## GOD'S PLAN FOR A FREE FUTURE

I grew up in a relatively healthy church, but I never understood when it came to money what I now know today about aligning my monetary resources with God's design and how that builds a foundation for a financially free future. It's my prayer that we all discover God-centered wisdom for living in every aspect of our lives, including money.

> What you truly believe about the nature and character of God directly impacts on your expectation to trust Him for increase

What you truly believe about the nature and character of God directly impacts on your expectation to trust Him for increase. Do you 'know' Him as completely good, as the One who bountifully blesses, who is powerfully able to do above and beyond? We need to change our thinking from a 'just give me enough to survive' mentality and reposition our thought patterns to align with God's word.

Considering again what the apostle Paul wrote in:

*2 Corinthians 9:8 And God is able to make all grace abound toward you, that you, always having all sufficiency in **all things**, may have an abundance for **every good work**.*

I would encourage you to read and ponder this verse every day for a week, allowing the Holy Spirit to speak to you. Every time I've spoken on this or read it for my own meditation, I find myself constantly challenged by it. 'God is able.' Your present circumstances do not inhibit God, neither do your past circumstances handicap Him. No. 'God is able to make all grace abound toward you.'

## INTERNAL ALIGNMENT PRECEDES EXTERNAL EVIDENCE

This is not a message for the person next to you. This is a message for you, it's a message for me. That this God is able to see us have all sufficiency in all things. Nothing excluded. 'That we may have an abundance for every good work.'

In other words, when you analyze the original text, we should all be living in a super-abounding kind of existence. Sure, we are faced with seasons of challenge, but our daily lives should be materially blessed, in order to bless those around us through our overflow. Many years ago this verse became the catalyst to prompting my commitment to search the scriptures to find out what I was missing and why. I had lived a generous life and yet still seemed to live continually limited within my financial world.

Something needed to change in me. I began to discover verses I had never seen before such as:

*3 John 2 Beloved, I pray that you may prosper in all things and be in health, just as your soul prospers.*

Being a Christian means you are a Christ follower. You have a personal relationship with Jesus, which continually increases your capacity to enable you to experience a bigger tomorrow. The commencement point is to allow the Holy Spirit, through God's word, to bring the adjustments that are needed. Our soul, which includes our thought processes, must transition to a commitment to prosper. In other words, internal alignment precedes external evidence.

---

## Internal alignment precedes external evidence

---

God is always bigger than the current challenges that are keeping us constrained. It is no small task to keep believing this, but His grace empowers us to commit to bring alignment of our thoughts to His ways. Without this, there will be no transformation.

## RESETTING SOVEREIGNTY – THE TITHE

Without even knowing it, in the early years of my life and Christian walk, at times I gave money to the Church out of a sense of obligation. Sometimes we can even give out of fear. I didn't want to live under a curse if I withheld, as was taught at the time, so I made sure I did what God's word told me to do.

Today I see this whole scenario in a totally different light and from a new perspective. I now understand that when money or the material world touches my life, my response determines who gains control. I am the one who gets to decide who gains the upper hand over my financial future. Sovereignty is about who has been given the reins, who has been positioned in the place of authority.

Tithing is about resetting sovereignty, and that leads us straight into this perplexing topic. The tithe is where we decide who becomes sovereign over our increase: God or mammon. Unlocking this principle will show us that whoever is placed over our 'first' has authority over the rest. Tithing is not just a Christian ritual or

## Whoever is placed over our 'first' has authority over the rest

something we do to pay the Church's bills. It encompasses so much more.

The media at times suggests churches make people tithe. If there is any truth in that statement, then this would be cultivating a misinterpretation of God's word. We have no right to manipulate people to do anything, but we will investigate how this principle is the foundation to the pathway for each of God's children to find financial release. I believe we need to be uncompromising in our conviction that 'the tithe' is God's, and it has never been ours.

It's worthwhile being reminded of Martin Luther's observation that: 'We cannot give God anything; for everything is already His, and all we have comes from Him. I can only give Him praise, thanks and honor.'

In the next chapter I explain how to live with authority over your money, rather than money ruling you. The most important aspect to understand in all of this conversation about finance is that it isn't really primarily about the money. It's about whose authority we position in our hearts that is outworked in our financial world.

# FOURTEEN

# TRUSTING GOD'S SOVEREIGNTY

You may be asking yourself how on earth you can afford to give God 10 percent of your increase – even if you wanted to – when you can barely make it through the week now. I want to assure you that the tithe was never established as a legalistic obligation. It's about you connecting with God's plan and acknowledging His sovereignty. Once we trust God fully in this area, we release His ability to take us on a journey through the financial maze of misunderstanding to a future of release.

Trusting in the infallibility of God's word is fundamental so that we do not give into confusion and disillusionment when we don't immediately experience a breakthrough.

I once heard a *Bible* teacher tell of a woman who saw tithing in a mistaken light. She marched up to the front of a church, put her hands on her hips, and said, 'I want my money back'. The leader asked, 'What are you talking about?' She said, 'I've been doing this for two weeks [speaking of tithing], and it doesn't work. I want my money back!' The woman was serious. She actually believed, like many Christians are seduced to do, that giving could buy her some kind of instant magic financial wand. You're not going to throw a little money in the church giving container and get your life that's been a mess for 20 or 30 years turned around in two weeks!

> **It's about you and me aligning with God and His sovereignty to begin to create a pathway into His promised blessing**

I'll emphasize the point again: it's about you and me aligning with God and His sovereignty to begin to create a pathway into His promised blessing.

## ARE YOU INSIDE OR OUTSIDE THE GARDEN?

From the beginning of time, there has always been a battle for sovereignty in play. Adam and Eve resided in the Garden of Eden, where they experienced full and unlimited provision. Within the garden was a significant tree, which I call the 'tree of choice' (the tree of the knowledge of good and evil), that Adam and Eve were forbidden to eat from. It was created by God for a specific reason. God in everything provides us with a choice; God desires a relationship that's freely offered and received, motivated purely by love – not one that functions out of fear or obligation.

Adam and Eve had a choice to trust Him, which determined whether they could walk closely in His presence or not. Sovereignty is not acquired by the demand 'you've got to do this or you'll be cursed'; it is 'I get to do this because I totally trust God, His promises for blessing and His plans for my life'.

Adam and Eve unfortunately made the wrong choice, disobeying God by eating the forbidden fruit, and were banished to life outside of the garden of paradise.

Could we apply this as a metaphor in the area of our finances? Although still His children, disobedience and lack of trust in God's word could position us outside the garden of His provision and protection.

The outcome of Adam and Eve's transgression was promised death. Even though they didn't die physically, they died to the wonder and the experience of God's relational proximity in their lives. It is amazing that their choices still impact us down through the generations. Through Jesus, however, we now have the opportunity to decide on our sovereignty and to not live with a 'banishment' mind-set when it comes to God's supply and defense of our finances. We can trust Him to restore all that was lost. Sovereignty is a decision of trust that brings God and His promises into full view.

> **Sovereignty is a decision of trust that brings God and His promises into full view**

## HOW WE HONOR GOD

God's word is so relevant to every one of us in this regard. It instructs us to:

**Proverbs 3:9** *Honor the LORD with your wealth, with the firstfruits of all your crops.* (NIV)

We are to honor the Lord. With what? With our worship? With our praise? Yes, but here the *Bible* says we are also to honor the Lord with our money and material things. Honor Him with our possessions, and with the firstfruits of all of our increase.

As author and pastor John Bevere says, 'True honor is an outflow from a heart that fears God' (*Honor's Reward*, FaithWords, 2007). When we get our wages, the first thing we do, not the second thing, not the ninth thing, is to say: 'Wow, I'm increasing. And

God, I choose to honor You and position You over my increase.'

Have we honored God in our increase? Is it our first response to do that? It is not when 'we feel the time is right' or based on 'if I can afford to do it'. No, this is a trust response, a faith response, a sovereignty response. One of the first and foremost things you do when positioning God as sovereign is bringing the first of your increase. If you do it with the first, the promise is God's increased blessing.

**Proverbs 3:9-10** *Honor the* LORD *with your possessions, and with the firstfruits of all your increase; so your barns will be filled with plenty, and your vats will overflow with new wine.*

## BUILDING AN INHERITANCE

In biblical times, barns were used to house the previous harvest, ready for the farmer's current need and also the seed for the next year's crop. Also, a portion of what was stored had a generational aspect to it, as it was stored up as an inheritance for future generations.

I believe we too should look at our material resources in exactly the same way. Imagine growing up in a society where our Christian forefathers, understanding this principle, had barns stored up ready for us. When we begin to realize that our decisions today are going to determine the platform of our children's children, the long-term impact of our obedience is highly significant.

> There's something about 'firsts' that gets God's attention

God always wants us to prepare the ground for the next generation. There's something about 'firsts' that gets God's attention.

Evangelist Billy Graham has said, 'If a person gets his attitude to money right, it will help straighten out almost every other area of his life.'

John D. Rockefeller Sr., one of America's wealthiest industrialists, saw the practical outworking of this principle in his life when he said: 'I never would have been able to tithe the first million dollars I ever made if I had not tithed my first salary, which was $1.50 per week.'

We'll take a closer look at just why the first is so precious and important in the next chapter, and how the principle of the first releasing the rest runs through the whole of scripture, from before the time of Abraham right through to Jesus and the first disciples.

# FIFTEEN

# RETURNING THE FIRST

---

Returning the first tenth to God determines and makes a statement about who has the authority over our lives. When it comes to our giving, heart attitude is all-important. If giving is undertaken with a spirit of honor and gratitude, instead of fearing the consequences if we don't obey, then God delights in responding. It's always your choice, but one that the *Bible* treats as of divine importance, as we will discover.

Billy Graham once said: 'One of our greatest sins is the fact that we are robbing God of what rightfully belongs to Him. When we don't tithe, we shirk a just debt. Actually you are not giving when we give God one tenth, because it already belongs to Him. This is a debt we owe. Not until we have given a tenth do we actually make an offering.'

Assuring that God has the 'first' from our increase is not only about positioning Him as Lord over all that we are and have but also about all that is coming our way in the future.

Some of you may protest: 'This firstborn stuff is all so Old Testament. It's not relevant for us today. We are covered by the New Covenant.'

It would be helpful to examine what the Old Testament law says on this topic. In *Exodus 13*, you find that the firstborn lamb was set aside to be offered. What was the reason for that? In biblical typology, this offering of the 'first' born was a forerunner to Christ's coming, the firstborn Son of God, offered for us. The first was always offered back to God. It is the pattern of God's provision for us: God gave His first Son. And His Son gave His life.

I want to propose a concept that goes beyond just an understanding of the principle of the 'first'. It is my conviction and my experience that the 'first releases the rest'. The enemy knows that if we get the priority of our tithe in order, it releases God to bless the remainder. The tithe was never to be an after-thought, or a last-minute option.

## The first releases the rest

No, it's a decision made before anything else happens. Because, as in Jesus, the first redeems the rest. The *Bible* says we love God because He first loved us. And in this narcissistic age of priority of self and dependence on self, unless we deliberately offer God the first of our increase, we are vulnerable to the relentless suggestion of the enemy to promote 'self' back in prime position.

## TWO BROTHERS, TWO OFFERINGS

*Genesis 4* is the story of two brothers, who both brought an offering to God. They were 'good guys'. Both brought up 'in the Church', they knew that God deserved an offering. The trouble started when it was only the younger of the two men, Abel, who received a positive response from the Lord. This outcome infuriated Cain, who was already angered at the rejection of his own gift.

The *Bible* says that, 'in the course of time', Cain brought his offering of 'some of the fruits' of the soil but Abel brought the 'fat portions' from the 'firstborn of his flock' (NIV). The implication is that Cain's offering was delayed and, we could even say, given out of obligation, while Abel's offering of 'fat portions' was one of abundance given out of an overflow of gratitude from his heart. Moreover, the fact that Abel's offering consisted of the firstborn of his flock suggests that he had pre-planned to offer this part of his flock to God and that he truly desired to give God the best that he could. In other words, Abel understood God's priority and gave with the right spirit while Cain's offering was tainted by obligation and wrong motives. God's challenge to Cain was that if he'd given in the correct method, he would have been blessed. From this example, we see God's favorable response to our first and our best that's given in faith, love and gratitude.

The tithe has always been about the first; it's never been about the second, third or fourth tenth, because this principle of positioning God as sovereign is so strong.

## TITHING – THE FOUNDATIONAL SCRIPTURE

The Old Testament prophet Malachi, writing in *Malachi 3*, provides us with a foundational scripture to help in understanding the tithing principle. And before you say 'that's Old Testament', let me state my case: yes, it is true – we do not live under the law; however, the Old Testament is filled with countless life lessons and truth that transforms. Have any of you rejected the validity of the Ten Commandments just because they are from the Old Testament? I would assume not. If you are of the opinion that the Old Testament is completely irrelevant, you may as well lose two thirds of the *Bible*. I think it would be wise to listen to the words of Jesus found in *Matthew*:

**Matthew 5:17-18** *Don't misunderstand why I have come. I did not come to abolish the law of Moses or the writings of the prophets. No, I came* *to accomplish their purpose. I tell you the truth, until heaven and earth disappear, not even the smallest detail of God's law will disappear until its purpose is achieved.* (NLT)

Jesus came and fulfilled Old Testament law and brought into play a new covenant; however, the Old Testament remains God's word and is far from irrelevant, as we will see below.

*Malachi 3:6-10 'For I am the LORD, I do not change; Therefore you are not consumed, O sons of Jacob. Yet from the days of your fathers you have gone away from My ordinances and have not kept them. Return to Me, and I will return to you,' says the LORD of hosts. 'But you said, "In what way shall we return?"'*

*'Will a man rob God? Yet you have robbed Me! But you say, "In what way have we robbed You?" In tithes and offerings. You are cursed with a curse, for you have robbed Me, even this whole nation. Bring all the tithes into the storehouse, that there may be food in My house, and try Me now in this,' says the LORD of hosts. 'If I will not open for you the windows of heaven and pour out for you such blessing that there will not be room enough to receive it.'*

Firstly, note the tone and the tense. 'For I am the LORD, I do not change. Therefore you are not consumed, O sons of Jacob. Yet from the days of your fathers you have gone away from My ordinances.'

It is very interesting that God begins by making reference to Himself and how His people had drifted away from Him and His ordinances. This was and is far more than an Old Testament law. 'I change not…' God is saying to them: this is about Me and who I am, not just what I want you to do. Allow me to paraphrase it: 'I am God and I never change and yet you have turned away from My laws, My ordinances, My statute, My way of living and from Me. These are the patterns, the structures that will release My authority over you. Yet you have gone away from them and you have not kept them.'

Note what God asks: 'Would you return to Me?' Not just 'Would you do what I ask, tick all the right boxes and simply fulfill My laws?' but also 'Would you return to Me?' This is very personal. 'And if you return to Me, then I will return to you. If you allow Me to be sovereign, then I will draw you into My proximity. But you said "In which way would we return to You?"'

The very next thing God says: 'Will a man rob God?...You say "In what way have we robbed you?"' God responds with, 'In tithes and offerings.'

Note that God separates the tithe and the offerings as they are very different. Many Christians fail to realize that this is not just about tithing but the giving of offerings as well. It is true that the tithe or the first tenth was required during the period of the Old Testament law but it also was offered before the law

> **God separates the tithes and offerings as they are very different**

was established and Jesus took time in *Matthew* to say we should continue in it.

Tithing:
- Is in the Old Testament *(Leviticus 27:30-32)*;
- Began before the law *(Genesis 14:18-20)*;
- Is required after the law *(Matthew 23:23)*.

## TITHING IS JUST THE BEGINNING

There are two considerations raised here. Firstly, that we are to return the tithe. And then we are to sow an offering when financial increase comes our way. God presents a test before us to choose His lordship first. Under the Old Testament law, failure to tithe and bring an offering meant you lived under a curse.

I personally believe that Jesus dealt with the curse in all shapes and forms at Calvary. So I don't believe, as I grew up accepting, that I will be cursed if I don't tithe. The way I understand it now is that if I choose not to embrace the ordinances of God and put Him as sovereign over my increase, then I live in a place of vulnerability outside of His provision and protection. When we fail to tithe and bring offerings, mammon has a right to take hold, and, yes, we are choosing to be financially independent from God, with the enemy having access to our resources.

This is such a major place of the enemy's attack, that I encourage you to choose God's blessing.

*Malachi 3:10* '*Bring all the tithes into the storehouse, that there may be food in My house, and try Me now in this,' says the* LORD *of hosts, 'If I will not open for you the windows of heaven and pour out for you such blessing that there will not be room enough to receive it.'*

Let's be clear around why God has instituted the tithe. The instruction is to bring all the tithes, the *Bible* says, into the storehouse – not to where we think we'd like to give them. It is not to our favorite charity, however needful it may be, or to the needs of others, missionaries or many other well-deserving causes. But into the storehouse – that is, the Church. As was evidenced in the statistics from the *Relevant* magazine report, this would make a most remarkable difference to our world as the Church was empowered to serve the needs and bring change in our societies.

---

The Church is God's primary vehicle to see His kingdom come on earth

---

Remember that the Church is God's primary vehicle to see His kingdom come on earth and He has instituted a plan for this to happen.

Not for a moment am I saying that we should not support great ministries and needs that are outside the Church, but that is for our offerings, not His tithe.

The scripture says: 'Try Me, test Me, prove Me'. We are all invited to bring God to the testing arena. He challenges us to test and try Him: 'And see if God will not open for you the windows of heaven. Pour out such a blessing that you cannot contain it. Then all the nations of the world will call you blessed' (paraphrased).

*Malachi 3:12 You'll be voted 'Happiest Nation'. You'll experience what it's like to be a country of grace.* (MSG)

God has always had a plan to fund His purpose and the enemy has always violently opposed it. Tithing is God's answer to the release of His provision for His church, to enable it to achieve His full intent here on earth. Again, remember: tithing began even before the law. In *Genesis 14:18-24* you'll read of Abram (430 years before Mosaic law – before he even became Abraham) tithing to Melchizedek, who was a forerunner, a shadow of Christ.

For me, tithing has never been an issue as, before I turned five, I was taught by my parents to honor God with the first tenth and, to be honest, sure I didn't understand it all but hand on heart, I can never remember a time where I haven't returned God's tithe on my increase. I have since discovered that tithing is the first element of a much fuller picture, which we will consider as we continue on.

# SIXTEEN

# WHAT JESUS SAID

---

If we choose to embrace the belief that tithing is no longer necessary for New Testament believers, it can lead to excuses such as 'God will understand if it's all a bit tough to give right now', even if it is genuinely true about our circumstances. We begin to reason with human logic and forfeit our trust in God's word. I wonder if you would concede that God knows best and our toughest season is exactly where His supernatural provision is needed.

Many years ago I was teaching a message on tithing in Sydney, and a dear lady who was a solo mum came to the front and said 'Oh, Pastor, that was so convicting, but I just can't afford to do this. I want to do it, but I've got the kids, and this is what's happened to me.' She went on to explain her financial situation and my heart just broke as it went out to her. To this day, I remember what I said to her, 'Look, it's OK; God understands. Just do what you can do.' Only to be in the car driving home around a half an hour later, and I felt the Holy Spirit begin to clearly challenge me: 'So you know better than Me, do you?' Seriously, I was shocked as all of a sudden I recognized that I had allowed my emotions to come before God's word. I had such a deep sense that I had misled her in what was God's best for her.

After that drive home with the Holy Spirit whispering to me, I felt deeply convicted again by the divine truth that nothing shifts unless God is positioned as sovereign. The weight of conviction was so strong that I couldn't do anything except ring the mother and apologize. I told her I had given her advice that came from a human perspective and no matter how hard it might be, if she honored God with the first, God had promised to bless. Obviously we also stepped in to help her with her current needs, as generosity is a kingdom value for all of us.

It may seem hard to trust God with your finances right now, but, remember, God said: 'Test Me. Prove Me. Try Me.' He said, if you put Him first, you will see how He would begin to step into the rest. Remember, Elijah told the widow who, with her son, was about to die because of lack of material provision, your answer lies in what you see as small, and utterly hopeless. Just mix that with the blessing of God and witness the eventual miracle.

## Your answer lies in what you see as small

### SO, WHAT WOULD JESUS SAY?

If you are one of those who say to themselves 'Jesus never taught tithing', I have to ask you: 'Take a closer look.' One of the foundational understandings of the first Christians was that tithing had always been right. Like we saw in *Malachi 3*, it is about who God is and it wasn't up for debate. It was foundational; it was what everybody did.

*Matthew 23:23* *What sorrow awaits you teachers of religious law and you Pharisees. Hypocrites! For you are careful to tithe even the tiniest income from your herb gardens, but you ignore the more important aspects of the law – justice, mercy, and faith. You should tithe, yes, but do not neglect the more important things.* (NLT)

Jesus was simply saying that the religious leaders were just ticking the boxes and fulfilling the principle of tithing, but they were far from pleasing God by doing it because of the attitude of their hearts. God wants our response to be heart driven. So, if you're reading this counsel about giving and it's eliciting a feeling of 'being controlled', then refrain from doing anything. You've got to respond out of a genuine heartfelt revelation.

Jesus tells them what was required (paraphrased): 'These you ought to have done. You ought to have tithed your increase. But not at the expense of leaving the other things – justice, mercy, faith – undone.'

## TITHING IS NOT AN 'OPTIONAL EXTRA'
Perhaps we'd take this instruction on tithing more seriously if we really understood how strong the *Bible* language is when it is discussed. To get some inkling of that, we need to turn to *John 3:1-21* and consider our friend Nicodemus.

He was an intelligent Pharisee with a genuine seeking heart. Despite all Nicodemus's knowledge about God, Jesus challenged the fact that he didn't know God intimately. 'You must be born again,' was His charge to him. Most of the Church today has no problem with this statement from Jesus. He said to Nicodemus: 'You can't just be a believer – you have to be born again, have a new birth experience!' In other words, if you allow God to forgive you, and do life God's way, then you will experience a brand-new life. That's standard theology, widely accepted.

But if we go back to the original Greek language for a moment, and take a look at that word 'must' that Jesus uses – 'you **must** be born again' – we find something very interesting. The same original Greek word for 'must' in 'you must be born again' is what Jesus uses when He says to the Pharisees (*Matthew 23:23*) that you '**ought** to have tithed'. It's not something that is to be seen as an optional extra. No, you 'must'; if you want God to be sovereign, break satan's stronghold in your material world by putting God first every time you increase. The ball is always in our court: who do we enthrone – God or mammon?

We could sum up by saying: the principle of tithing began before the law, was embraced by God in the Mosaic law, and then sanctioned by Jesus in the New Testament. It is founded upon an act of worship and dedication to God. It recognizes and positions lordship and recognizes the priority God places on His house.

The great evangelist Charles Haddon Spurgeon spoke of his experience in living under God's sovereignty when he said: 'In all of my years of service to my Lord, I have discovered a truth that has never failed and has never been compromised. That truth is that it is beyond the realm of possibilities, that one has the ability to out-give God. Even if I give the whole of my worth to Him, He will find a way to give back to me much more than I gave.'

> It is beyond the realm of possibilities, that one has the ability to out-give God

We will move on to examining the blessings and benefits we come into when we choose to make God sovereign in our lives by outlining a first key reason we choose to tithe.

# SEVENTEEN

# LIVING UNDER GOD'S SOVEREIGNTY

You might sympathize with author Shane Claiborne, who, in *The Irresistible Revolution*, recalls seeing an old comic strip 'that had two guys talking to each other, and one of them says he has a question for God. He wants to ask why God allows all of this poverty and suffering to exist in the world. And his friend says, "Well, why don't you ask Him?" The fellow shakes his head and says he is too scared. When his friend asks why, he mutters "I'm scared God will ask me the same question."'

I admit I've felt the same way. Over and over, when I ask God why all the poverty and injustices exist in the world, I can feel the Spirit whisper to me, 'YOU tell ME'. If we got hold of, and were faithful as God's children to, the ordinance of tithing and giving offerings, the Church would be positioned to become the hope

**As we return what belongs to God, we release His blessing over the remaining 90 percent**

of the world, bringing an answer to need.

Rather than taking the viewpoint that you are 'paying your tithe', consider things from a different perspective. As we return what belongs to God, we release His blessing over the remaining 90 percent.

## TITHING DETERMINES SOVEREIGNTY

I hope you are beginning to see that the first reason I tithe is to establish God's sovereignty in my life. He will always be God, but I get to choose whether I am lorded over by mammon or released by El Shaddai; whether I'm robbing Him of access into my 'today' and my 'tomorrow'.

Of course, you can do life without living under the rule of God for a season and perhaps even be oblivious to that reality; but when the enemy strikes, we need to have God as our protector and provider. The tithe was and is non-negotiable. Every point of our increase carries the challenge to return to God what is His.

***Leviticus 27:30*** *All the tithe of the land, whether of the seed of the land or of the fruit of the tree, is the LORD'S. It is holy to the LORD.*

That's why I don't pay MY tithe; I return the Lord's tenth. That is a big difference. The tithe is and has always been holy. It's a principle, it's not a law, and it's holy. Let me break down that thought. It is 'holy to the LORD'. What does holy mean? What does holy look like?

Back in *Leviticus*, if you kept the tithe to pay it later, you had to add the accrued interest to it, because God was teaching His people the tithe didn't belong to them. The principle today remains the same. The curse has been broken, but the holiness of the tithe prevails. The word 'holy' comes from the Hebrew word 'qodesh', which literally means 'something that is separated, sacred and consecrated'.

God is holy and He calls His tithe holy. God is saying: This isn't even about money; this isn't about the needs of the Church: this is about Me. The question we have to answer is, does holy ever change? Of course it doesn't, as holiness is an attribute of God, who is the same yesterday, today and forever.

Over many years numbers of people have said to me, 'We don't believe in tithing. We just give, and I often give more than the tithe. I give how I feel to give.' I wouldn't be that trusting of human nature. Think about it: if you or I were to live out what we feel at times, where would we end up? If we were to build anything on how we feel, we would ultimately end up in crisis.

We can't afford to allow what is holy to be subjected to what is human. Remember, the first 10 percent of all our increase is God's and the remaining 90 percent is entrusted to our own stewardship decisions.

> Tithing is about the reinstating, the resetting of sovereignty

Tithing is about the reinstating, the resetting of sovereignty. It doesn't matter who you are; it's about a decision based on God's word.

## WHEN CHAOS COMES, GOD WILL BE THERE

There is a story from the life of Elijah the Prophet in *1 Kings 17:7-24* that illustrates this point perfectly.

*1 Kings 17:8 Then the word of the LORD came to him, saying, 'Arise, go to Zarephath… and dwell there. See, I have commanded a widow there to provide for you.'*

Understanding that the land was experiencing severe famine gives some context to this narrative. Elijah was a man with a price on his head, hunted by the wicked Queen Jezebel. In Zarephath, a poor widow lived with her only son, making preparation for their final meal before they starved to death. God tells Elijah to go to her house and ask her for a meal. God tells Elijah that He has commanded a widow to supply him with food.

Elijah arrives and asks her: 'Please, bring me a little water in a cup that I may drink.' As she sets off to fetch it, he calls to her and adds 'Oh, and while you are at it, please bring me also a morsel of bread.' (More or less!)

She replies: 'As the LORD your God lives, I do not have bread, only a handful of flour in a bin, and a little oil in a jar; and see, I am gathering a couple of sticks that I may go in and prepare it for myself and my son, that we may eat it, and die.'

Elijah says to her: 'Do not fear; go and do as you have said, but make me a small cake from it first [God's principle – the first releases the rest] and afterward make some for yourself and your son.'

It is very important that we understand God was not sending Elijah to this widow so she could supply food for him. He was sending Elijah (who also represents the Word of God, the plan of God, the purpose of God) to bring a miracle and an answer to her prayer.

## GOD IS NEVER NOT THERE

The principle of sovereignty and lordship reveals to us that even when we face drought and famine, God is there. He has never ever not been there. This is what Elijah is saying to the widow when he tells her that if she does as he asks and feeds him first: 'The bin of flour shall not be used up nor shall the jug of oil run dry until the day the LORD sends rain on the earth.'

When God gets the first, He's released to work a miracle with the rest. It's amazing how the enemy uses fear to cause us to distrust the Word of God, and once we accept his lies, we never seem to get off the roundabout of restriction and lack. Our lack is often rooted in our lack of obedience. As for the widow…

*1 Kings 17:15-16 So she went away and did according to the word of Elijah; and she and he and her household ate for many days. The bin of flour was not used up, nor did the jar of oil run dry, according to the word of the LORD which He spoke by Elijah.*

So, what is my first reason to tithe? I tithe because it establishes God's sovereignty over my life. I don't want my own ability, the current economic climate, or anything of the enemy to determine my future. I want God to reign supreme. And when I position Him as Lord, He has the authority to fashion my future.

> Our lack is often rooted in our lack of obedience

## GOD DOESN'T NEED YOUR MONEY

By the way, we've said it before but it's worth reiterating: God doesn't need your money. He'll use it, but He doesn't need it. *Malachi 3:6-8* makes it very clear: it's not my tithe – it is returning to God what is His.

The tithe is many things:
- It is non-negotiable.
- It is to be given first, before anything else is kept for oneself.
- It releases lordship.
- It is an ordinance more than a law.
- It establishes divine release once returned.
- It has never been seed.
- It is holy.

*Haggai 2:8 'The silver is Mine, and the gold is Mine', says the LORD of hosts.*

It is so much more than money itself. It's about something so much deeper – it's the first. It's about access and authority.

Remember how the Israelites were promised Canaan? And so they went to Canaan, and the first big acquisition was to overtake Jericho. God promised to be with them but directed them not to collect any of the spoils.

Achan (recorded in *Joshua* 7) disobeyed the Lord and, after the victory, snatched some of the plunder. The result of his disobedience and the way he dishonored God's word meant impending judgement over all of Israel. The next time they went to war they were defeated at Ai. That's how important it is to be obedient to God's word.

Some of us are living without God's hand over our material world, because we haven't honored God with the first of our increase. Robbing (according to *Malachi* 3) means to have something in our possession that doesn't belong to us. It doesn't hurt to stop sometimes and ask ourselves 'Have I really been faithful with everything I have increased by?'

> Have I really been faithful with everything I have increased by?

Remember, *Malachi* is the only place, from the beginning of *Genesis* to the end of *Revelation*, where God says: 'You put Me to the test. You prove Me. Trust Me and you will see what I can do with the 90 percent.' So why not do it? As you'll discover more fully in the next chapter, tithing not only establishes God's sovereignty and authority over your life but on a deeper level it also helps future-proof your life.

# EIGHTEEN

# FUTURE-PROOFING
# YOUR LIFE

I think it would be true to say that unless God is front and center of all our financial affairs, they remain vulnerable. Our resources will be prone to decay and destruction. It is imperative that we become aware of the amount of time, attention and emotion that we devote and expend on money matters and the acquisition of material assets.

**Matthew 6:21** *Where your treasure is, there your heart will be also.*

Where your heart is, your actions and your life will follow. One of the assurances given in scripture is that your life will follow the state of your heart. That is why our lives must be lived out from a God-centered revelation. The difference between Christianity and religion is that religion demands all types of external behaviors, whereas God works to transform your inner world as your heart remains the engine room of your life.

At the center of all this talk about *God Money & Me* are these words

**Your heart remains the engine room of your life**

of Jesus in *Matthew*, which, when translated, could read: 'Did you realize that you can future-proof your life? And this is how you would do it: you make the right heart decisions about money.' In effect, 'Where your money is, your heart will be, and where your heart is, you will follow.' This is a profound thought, and I don't want us to lose its true impact. Often we don't stop long enough to pull back the covers and get a real revelation of what this means.

## SOVEREIGNTY'S DEEPEST SIGNIFICANCE

We are entering deep waters here, because in this whole issue of sovereignty, we discover that what we honor has the authority to rule us. We are told that the tithe is holy *(Leviticus 27:30)*. That means literally hallowed, dedicated, sacred to God. Retaining the tithe in our own possession is akin to keeping hold of something that is not rightfully ours.

**Retaining the tithe in our possession is akin to keeping hold of something that is not rightfully ours**

The respected theologian A.W. Tozer has observed: 'I do not think I exaggerate when I say that some of us put our offering in the plate with a kind of triumphant bounce as much as to say: "There – now God will feel better!" I am obliged to tell you that God does not need anything you have. He does not need a dime of your money. It is your own spiritual welfare at stake in such matters as these. You have the right to keep what you have all to yourself – but it will rust and decay, and ultimately ruin you.'

I've been in the Church from the time I was born, so people naturally do ask 'Well, what have been the keys to successful Christian living?' There are many keys, but one of the things

I've realized, looking back, is that I have always put God first financially by returning His tithe.

A.W. Tozer summarized it like this: 'The man who has God for his treasure has all things in one.'

## RESETTING AUTHORITY

As we have discussed, the tithe is the simple act of honoring God by returning the first of our increase to Him and releasing His blessing on the rest. And we've seen that if we are obedient to His financial instructions, we will have the key to international renewal and 'have an abundance for every good work'.

*Proverbs 3:9* *Honor the Lord with your possessions, and with the firstfruits of all your increase.*

Let's look at this very practically. When we receive our salary, that constitutes increase. If we receive a gift, an inheritance or even when we sell something for more than we bought it for, that equates to increase. Say you buy a house for $400,000 and you spend $50,000 on renovating it. After some time you sell it for $650,000. Your increase would amount to $200,000. Our increase reflects what we are to return. All increase is to be tithed on, and so honor God.

Material things so easily grab our hearts. No matter how hard it may seem, God's divine way will bless you in the long term.

*Malachi 3:10* *[I will] open for you the windows of heaven and pour out for you such blessing that there will not be room enough to receive it.*

Getting a sound hold on this principle will change the financial platform of the generations that follow us. Every time we declare the lordship and sovereignty of God by tithing, we are breaking any stronghold the enemy may have over our money. Tithing is all about resetting sovereignty over our material world.

# NINETEEN

# RELEASING GOD INTO OUR FUTURE

---

We've been building a picture of what it means to 'honor God with our possessions and firstfruits'. I hope you are getting a big, global sense of just how important this principle is.

---

**Full honor activates full release**

---

To put it in the language we have been using, 'full honor activates full release'. And practically speaking, there are four stages we need to follow through on if we're going 'get it right' and build the plan of God into our financial future.

## ESTABLISH GOD'S SOVEREIGNTY

Before we move on, let's briefly recap what we've established:

- We choose to make God sovereign by returning His tithe. **Haggai 2:8** *The silver is Mine, and the gold is Mine.*
- Jesus uses the same word for a 'compelling action' for both His instruction to Nicodemus that if he wants eternal life he must be born again *(John 3:1-21)* and His instruction to

the Pharisees that they ought to tithe *(Matthew 23:23)*.

- Once ownership of the tithe has been established, God's blessing is released over the remaining 90 percent.

## ESTABLISH GOD'S HOUSE

The tithe also resources God's house, the Church – His primary chosen expression of His kingdom. Let's just remind ourselves: the tithe was for the storehouse.

In *Malachi 3:10-12*, remember, God asks us to: 'bring all the tithes into the storehouse, that there may be food [my paraphrasing – resource, provision] in My house. . . And all nations will call you blessed, for you will be a delightful land.'

The storehouse is a place of protection, discipline, care, responsibility and 'more than enough'. Over my lifetime, I've witnessed the adversary's strategy in seeking to weaken and divide the Church. Without doubt, she will always be God's number-one plan for this earth – full stop! She is the bride of Jesus even with all her imperfections. By not understanding the purpose of our Church, we end up supplying arms to the enemy and aiding him in his agenda to ensure that she never realizes her full potential.

Once we all obey God's word by living His plan to bring His tithe into the storehouse, we will see it become a place of comfort, forgiveness, hope, vision and provision for many.

## DON'T LIVE SMALL

There is little argument that vision requires provision. Without the release of provision, vision remains merely a dream.

*Psalm 37:22* *Those blessed by Him shall inherit the earth.*

Let's all make a commitment to not live small. Our best days are ahead. All of us become enlarged when we lift our perspective

## Without the release of provision, vision remains merely a dream

from just enough to more than enough.

*Psalm 37:23-25* *The steps of a good man are ordered by the LORD, and He delights in his way. Though he fall, he shall not be utterly cast down; for the LORD upholds him with His hand. I have been young, and now am old; yet I have not seen the righteous forsaken, nor his descendants begging bread.*

The enemy wants to keep you and God's house malnourished. If you live malnourished for too long, you become sterile. However, once we begin to bring an answer to our world, God's kingdom begins to shine.

### INVOKE GOD'S PROVISION AND PROTECTION

It's simple but it's challenging. When we go through the tough times, God says: 'I'll protect you through them.' Paul made this statement:

*Philippians 4:13* *I can do all things through Christ who strengthens me.*

We often don't think about what led him to that point.

*Philippians 4:11-12* *I have learned in whatever state I am, to be content. I know how to be abased, and I know how to abound.*

Whether you have abundance or whether you find yourself with lack – which is why this subject of *God Money & Me* is so important. In fact, true prosperity is when you know God's blessing is with you despite your current circumstances. Paul was saying, 'I have to come to grips with the fact that, even in the toughest times, God's protection is around me and God's provision is with me no matter how my today may seem. Therefore I can stand in the eye of the storm, remain faithful and prove God in everything.'

> I can stand in the eye of the storm, remain faithful and prove God in everything

Will you prove God? It begins with the first tenth, trusting God enough to return what belongs to Him.

It may take a while to get out of debt, and we'll talk about that later, but let me seriously encourage you. The best days of your life are ahead if you honor God and reset His sovereignty every time you increase. Your children's children will thank God for your obedience.

In the next couple of chapters I want to look at the twelve ways we limit financial growth.

# TWENTY

# FACTORS LIMITING FINANCIAL GROWTH: ONE-SIX

---

I don't think I ever heard a message in my early Church life about money and how it works. All I heard was let's all keep sowing and let's be generous. I love that, but I never understood that you could give generously and yet still limit financial blessing. Let's take a look at some of the factors that limit our financial blessing.

## ONE – WHEN WE FAIL TO POSITION GOD AS SOVEREIGN OVER OUR INCREASE

As we have seen, when we honor God by returning what is holy, we release God's ability to breathe on and bless the rest.

## TWO – WHEN WE DON'T SOW FOR HARVEST

It came as a real surprise to me when I realized my tithe was not seed. In scripture, the tithe is never called seed or confused with seed. We need God's hand on our finances but also there is a need to create harvest through the sowing of seed.

*2 Corinthians 9:6-7* *But this I say: He who sows sparingly will also reap sparingly, and he who sows bountifully will also reap bountifully. So let each one give as he purposes in his heart, not grudgingly or of necessity; for God loves a cheerful giver.*

We all agree that harvest is the outcome of seed; in fact, every farmer sows because they expect to see a harvest. This is a divine law. Once we have honored God by returning what is His, we then activate this principle of sowing and reaping. Not just sowing but also sowing with an expectation of increase. This is an area where I had to make big changes in myself, because I grew up in a culture of 'Don't ask for more: be happy with what you've got.'

My parents often reminded me that 'they never had what I had'. Of course it is good to be grateful for what we do have, but to live with this limited mind-set is not what God wants. The *Bible* says if you sow, you have a right to expect harvest.

## If you sow, you have a right to expect harvest

So when I sow, like every farmer, I am to believe there's going to be a harvest.

*Proverbs 11:24-25* *There is one who scatters, yet increases more […] The generous soul will be made rich, and he who waters will also be watered himself.*

This again reflects the eternal law that more comes with sowing. Seeding with an expectation of reaping means that we're going to look for God to turn up and respond to our seed. I continually had to challenge the mind-sets I had developed through years of sitting under teaching that never encouraged an expectation of gathering

## We must embrace the law of sowing and reaping

more. Let me assure you that receiving is not wrong; God wants us to increase our ability in this area so we can have a greater answer for the need we are surrounded with. We must embrace the law of sowing and reaping.

## THREE – WHEN WE ACCOMMODATE DESTRUCTIVE DEBT

Some people would teach what I believe to be an extreme: that all debt is wrong. I do believe we need to understand debt and be careful with it. Whenever our debt has the decision-making ability over us, it's out of order because it has accessed the place of authority.

I would say it is unwise to go into debt for any depreciating asset. You say, 'But I want the latest TV, car, phone, fridge like my best friend/brother/neighbor.' If it's to buy something that is depreciating, I would urge you not to go into debt for it. When Maree and I were first married we made a decision that we would first recover what we had spent on our wedding before we bought what we thought we needed. Today we are reaping the benefit of not becoming strangled by destructive debt.

**Proverbs 22:7** *The rich rules over the poor, and the borrower is servant to the lender.*

I don't think it's necessarily wrong to borrow for an appreciating asset. Most of us do that with homes. But we must really be careful and understand the wisdom of delayed gratification. In some countries you can fund your college or university education with an interest-free loan, but be aware that you can't evade that debt forever – it becomes attached to your life. I'm not saying it is a bad idea, but when debt gets to a place where it is our decision-maker, it will damage the purposes of God. Again I am not suggesting borrowing for study is misguided; however, I am cautioning against letting debt rule us. Remember what the *Bible* says: the one who borrows ends up a servant.

## FOUR – WHEN WE DON'T EMBRACE A STRONG WORK ETHIC

For me, this would be a very big part of creating a financial future. Did you know that faith demands work? Every level of higher faith requires an equal level of personal commitment. *James* teaches us that if we want to live with big faith and big vision, we need to be fully involved. You may feel God's not blessing you – and what are you doing about that?

*James 2:14 What does it profit, my brethren, if someone says he has faith but does not have works? Can faith save him?*

We all get 168 hours every week. If you need 8 hours a night to sleep, then over 7 days you'll spend 56 hours sleeping. That means there's 112 left. You need to eat, connect with others, spend time with God and enjoy all He has for us and work. Very simply, if we are lacking the needed funds, we may for a season need to turn the TV and social media off, and work a second job. Sound a bit too practical?

I come from a Dutch background. I can't really remember a time in my life when I haven't worked at least one and a half lots of 40-hour weeks. Most of my life I've worked the equivalent of two working weeks in one week. It may be that is the way I'm wired but it is also the way I was taught. The truth is, it hasn't killed me. It's released me. We have all got 112 waking hours at our discretion every week. You say 'You're being hard.'

*Proverbs 6:6-11 Go to the ant, you sluggard! Consider her ways and be wise, which, having no captain, overseer or ruler, provides her supplies in the summer, and gathers her food in the harvest. How long will you slumber, O sluggard? When will you rise from your sleep? A little sleep, a little slumber, a little folding of the hands to sleep – so shall your poverty come on you like a prowler, and your need like an armed man.*

Goodness, those ants are busy, aren't they? When was the last time you stopped and just watched them for ten minutes with the intention of finding wisdom? You will discover they have no captain, they have no overseer, no ruler. But they provide their supplies in the summer and they gather their food in the harvest. 'How long will you slumber, O sluggard? . . A little sleep, a little slumber, a little folding of the hands and poverty will come on you like a prowler.'

The truth is, a release in finance involves both what God needs to do and what we need to do.

**Proverbs 22:29** *Do you see a man who excels in his work? He will stand before kings.*

Once we embrace the level of our responsibility, we will often be the first to work and the last to leave. Promotion will be on the horizon when we live this kind of attitude. You may say 'Yeah, it's all right for you, but I haven't been able to get a job for a while.'

Do you know I've never been out of work? Let me explain. There have been times I couldn't get work, but I've never been out of work. If you haven't got a job, make a decision that you will work anyway – money or not. Don't sit at home watching *Coronation Street* or *Game Of Thrones*. You may find these statements a little confronting, but I am hoping my 'tough love' will be of assistance.

Out of work? Yes, work for free. Don't know what to do? Well, what would you like to do? Identify a company you would like to join and offer to do whatever is needed, without pay, for a month.

---

**Out of work? Yes, work for free**

---

Get involved in a charity you want to help. Turn up at church and say 'I'm out of work at the moment, I can't get a job. I'm here to work, no strings attached.'

While you're volunteering, don't turn up at midday and leave at 1:30pm. When do you work? Ask what hours people work and if the response is, '8:30am till 5:00pm', turn up at 8:15am, ask for something to do, and stay till 5:30pm. If you have that kind of attitude, there will be a breakthrough over time.

**Proverbs 20:4** *The lazy man will not plow because of winter; he will beg during harvest and have nothing.*

There is no excuse. We as Christians should be amongst the hardest of workers.

## FIVE – WHEN WE HAVE NO DEVELOPING INVESTMENT PLAN

To live a financially balanced life and therefore experience God's blessing, we need a holistic view. I have made reference to the fact that my dad never really understood this. In fact, I can recall him saying to me: 'Son, I began with nothing and it did me no harm, and the same goes for you.' Like every other area of our lives, our financial management requires intentionality and longevity. I will have much more to say about this in the following chapters. I think for many generations the overarching thinking has been, 'Well, Jesus is coming soon'. In other words, 'No need to think generationally.' This is absolutely foreign to a biblical pattern.

> Everything about today's decisions should lead towards releasing a benefit in our tomorrow

**Proverbs 13:22** *A good man leaves an inheritance to his children's children.*

I believe that everything about today's decisions should lead towards releasing a benefit in our tomorrow. This is true in our financial world, as in everything else. So the question is: do you have an investment plan?

## SIX – WHEN WE UNWISELY GIVE EVERYTHING AWAY

I've mentioned already how a number of times Maree and I gave everything away in the first 15 years of marriage. We don't live with regrets, but today I realize that we often responded primarily out of the emotion of the moment. Yes, I do believe that at times God asks us to sacrifice and do extraordinary things. But equally I believe we are called to create an inheritance for our children's children. Again, we will look at how we can live a generous life and build an increasing financial future by embracing the **'10/10/10/80 PRINCIPLE'** in Part Five of *God Money & Me*.

# TWENTY-ONE

# FACTORS LIMITING FINANCIAL GROWTH: SEVEN-TWELVE

Having pastored a large church family for many years and having been committed to see people reach their full potential, I have encouraged many to embrace a mind-set of never arriving. There is always something we can develop and do better, as we all live with blind spots. Let's look at some further areas that can limit financial release.

## SEVEN – WHEN WE REFUSE FINANCIAL ACCOUNTABILITY

Good decisions are managed decisions. Why is it that we're happy for other people to speak into most other areas of our lives, but not in regard to finance? I would suggest that if we don't have an openness for people to see what we do with our finances, there's a deeper issue that needs to be attended to.

> Good decisions are managed decisions

I'm not saying to show the world, but we all need to find people whom we trust and who are advanced in their skills and thinking in this area. Like a sports coach, as soon as they see a fault or weakness in our game, they say 'That's creeping in; let's address that.'

Accountability ensures we keep true to what we set out to achieve in the first place.

**Proverbs 11:14** *Where there is no counsel, the people fall.*

When it comes to tithing and giving, let's not see it as an obligation but as a joy, realizing the enemy will do everything to stop or divert us. That's because once we become obedient, we release so much. We release God's authority into our financial worlds, as well as freeing up what we need personally, creating an abundance for every good work, and provisioning the generations to follow.

**Psalm 112:1-3** *Praise the LORD! Blessed is the man who fears the LORD, who delights greatly in His commandments. His descendants will be mighty on earth; the generation of the upright will be blessed. Wealth and riches will be in his house, and his righteousness endures forever.*

If you don't have some form of management and accountability, you will end up drifting because of circumstantial and enemy pressure. The whole paradigm (paraphrased) is: 'Blessed is the man who fears the Lord, who is under the lordship, the boundaries of God.' And that's all about management.

EIGHT – WHEN WE BUY INTO A 'GET RICH QUICK' LIE
The next email you get from some unknown source about a financial scheme that seems too good to be true, press 'delete'. Seriously, I am not sure how many Christians I know who have fallen prey to a 'get rich quick' lie. Many have even said they were praying for a breakthrough when this opportunity came. My perspective is that anything that seems too good to be true is

too good to be true. Ultimately how to build your way into a strong financial future is not in a one-off situation but by God-centered principled living. What can be gained overnight can be lost overnight.

## What can be gained overnight can be lost overnight

There was a time when we lived in Sydney when many people in the wider Church body were approached by some developers of a new invention. Many invested all their savings into this new project that was going to change the world. Unfortunately the whole thing fell over, and the resulting outcome was that many people got hurt, some even blaming God. God is a principled God and builds every area of our lives, line upon line.

*Proverbs 28:19 He who tills his land will have plenty of bread, but he who follows frivolity will have poverty enough! A faithful man will abound with blessings, but he who hastens to be rich will not go unpunished.*

## NINE – WHEN WE NO LONGER GIVE TO THE POOR
God is passionate about those that become trapped in their struggle. The increasing strength of our financial position is to enable us to meet the needs of the poor more fully. Some say they don't believe in a handout but a hand up. I believe in both a handout and a hand up. We should all help people; we should be known for the generosity of the kingdom. Consider:

*Proverbs 19:17 He who has pity on the poor lends to the LORD.*

*Psalm 41:1 Blessed is he who considers the poor; the LORD will deliver him in time of trouble.*

## TEN – WHEN WE GO GUARANTOR FOR A FRIEND

I had never really heard this preached. I've seen it in scripture but the more you look into it, the more you see that many have fallen into a financial trap because they failed to live this.

*Proverbs 6:1-5* (paraphrased) makes it clear: 'My son, if you become guarantor for your friend, if you've shaken hands in pledge for a stranger, you are snared by the words of your mouth and you are taken by the words of your mouth. Do not sleep tonight, but get out of that contract.'

Why? I think because when we act as guarantor for a friend or someone in our world and it doesn't work out for them, we lose the money and the friendship. I also think the other side of it is: when we act as guarantor for someone that the banks won't go guarantor for, quite possibly we're setting them up for something before they're ready. If you ever become a guarantor for somebody, don't get angry with God or angry with them if it falls over and you lose everything, because the *Bible* teaches not to do it.

## ELEVEN – WHEN WE ALLOW MONEY TO DETERMINE OUR DECISIONS

This thought should be a book in itself, as most people often fall into this financial snare. You get a tempting job offer that requires you to move cities. It must be from God, right? Because it looks so promising and the money is so good. The question remains: is God the author of our major decisions or is money the decision-maker?

**Proverbs 11:28** *He who trusts in his riches will fall, but the righteous will flourish like foliage.*

I have come to realize that there would be many people who'd make a major change for better money, who would not seriously ask God first. You're not going to see the multiplying power of God when money is the base that determines your actions. Remember, money will come to you when you are in what God wants to do.

## TWELVE – WHEN WE FORGET THAT PERSEVERANCE CREATES A PATHWAY

I hope you are beginning to see that to live under a canopy of God's blessing financially, there are many contributing factors involved. I believe we are about to head into the most exciting part of the book as we discover practical keys to create a financial future.

However, we all need to understand and activate perseverance.

**Proverbs 20:4** *The lazy man will not plow because of winter; he will beg during harvest and have nothing.*

You are the city on a hill *(Matthew 5:14-16)*. Some of us wouldn't even be willing to walk up the hill because it's too much hard work. Some of us would never see ourselves being positioned on a hill, let alone owning a hill. And if the enemy can keep you bound by where you are today, he can keep you from God's promised outcome.

> If the enemy can keep you bound by where you are today, he can keep you from God's promised outcome

If you persevere with what God says, you will become a testimony of how God stepped in and brought multiplication to you and through you. In Part Four – Money's Release – we will dig a little deeper into the principles the *Bible* provides for in building a balanced financial future. We will talk about how God's bountiful provision is not just so you can feel happy and satisfied, but so you can also channel His blessing to others. You are 'blessed to be a blessing'.

# MONEY'S TEST

_____

Every one of us, if we align our material increase with God's plan, can build a foundation to a financially free future. One of the cornerstones for that is the returning of the first 10 percent to its owner: God. Choosing to put God first in our finances releases His sovereignty over everything else materially in our lives, because the first releases the rest.

Our attitude and obedience towards honoring God first is a matter of divine importance. It ensures mammon has no hold, but, more importantly, it releases God's blessing over our material world and financial future.

## MAIN REFLECTION POINTS:

1.  Write out *Malachi 3:6-10.*

2.  Why do you think tithing is such a challenge for many Christians?

3.  What is the first reason we tithe?

4. Create a list of the ways in which you see increase *(Proverbs 3:9).*

5. Out of the twelve limitors to financial growth, list the three that have affected you the most.

6.  Write out what your biggest personal revelation is from Part
    Three of *God Money & Me*.

7.  According to *Malachi 3*, where does God's tithe belong?
    Explain why you think God decided that.

# PART FOUR
# MONEY'S RELEASE

# TWENTY-TWO

# BLESSED TO BE A BLESSING

O nce we've understood the principle of the first and God's sovereignty, we are ready to gain extra insights around the subject of freeing abundance.

I have no doubt God loves to bless His children; however, I wholeheartedly agree with pastor and author Rick Warren when he said 'We are blessed not just so that we can feel good, not just so we can be happy and comfortable, but so that we will bless others. "We are blessed to be a blessing."' God told Abram:

**We are blessed to be a blessing**

*Genesis 12:2 I will make you into a great nation. I will bless you and make you famous, and you will be a blessing to others.* (NLT)

When considering the blessing of God, we firstly note that: it blesses us on its way to others. We are never the only destination point, but a channel through which money and material blessing flow for God's purposes.

## MONEY – THE YET-TO-BE-RELEASED MIRACLE

We have established previously that God's kingdom includes blessing of material wealth. Yet our lack of activating biblical revelation will often account for the reason why we are living with financial limitation. No matter how well intentioned you may be, your reality could be that you are yet to see the miracle of monetary release. Now that we've established the priority of the tithe, in the following chapters I want to explore further insights to creating ongoing financial freedom.

Maree and I were a classic example of two people who decided from the time we were married to commit to living generous lives. We categorically believed that God was true to His word and that harvest was the result of seed. I remember making a commitment together that we would, over a five-year period, increase our giving every year. The fifth year we were giving 37 percent of our gross income away. We love to give and it was amazing to see how God provided for many immediate needs we had personally. What didn't seem to add up was that after 15 years of marriage, we still had no major material assets and the prospect of ever buying a home was simply out of the equation.

This was when, for the first time, I realized that tithing and giving were not revealing the full blueprint of how God would direct us to creating a pathway to financial freedom. *God Money & Me* is the outcome of our discovery. Our question was simple: how do we continue to honor God, be generous and yet build a financial future for ourselves and the generations to follow?

You may find yourself in that very same position. The great news is that we discovered what I believe were the missing elements and it all began with a shift of understanding. For many people, even to believe that their personal financial world could change will also take a complete transformation in thinking.

*Proverbs 8:17-21* *I love those who love me, and those who seek me diligently will find me. Riches and honor are with me, enduring riches and righteousness. My fruit is better than gold, yes, than fine gold, and my revenue than choice silver. I traverse the way of righteousness, in the midst of the paths of justice, that I may cause those who love me to inherit wealth, that I may fill their treasuries.*

Wow, what a promise! Maree and I had always understood that God is good and yet our view of what was needed had been so confined. In the fifth and final part of *God Money & Me* we will paint the full picture of what has brought a release in the area of our finances.

Remember, the starting point is that when we honor God in the first place, it is then that we position ourselves to unlock the blessing of an all able and loving God.

*Proverbs 3:9-10* *Honor the LORD with your possessions, and with the firstfruits of all your increase; so your barns will be filled with plenty, and your vats will overflow with new wine.*

## DON'T SETTLE IN SMALL-MINDEDNESS

God's release is for far more than just personal blessing. It offers us liberty in every area of our lives, and constructs the right foundations for establishing a generational blessing. *Psalm 112* captures this sense of the abundant life God has planned for us when the psalmist cries in joy:

*Psalm 112:1-3* *Praise the LORD. Blessed are those who fear the LORD, who find great delight in His commands. Their children will be mighty in the land; the generation of the upright will be blessed. Wealth and riches are in their houses, and their righteousness endures forever.* (NIV)

> ## God's release... constructs the right foundations for establishing a generational blessing

Notice that here we see wealth and righteousness coupled together. God continues to enlarge our understanding of who He is and how He has called us to live. There's no implication in the above scripture that it's somehow questionable for a Christian to experience material blessing.

I was 38 years old before the foundational verses of God's plan for our money really began to come alive to me. We've probably all read them many times, but I fear that, for many of us, just like it was for me, we fail to grasp their true significance.

*2 Corinthians 9:8* God is able to make all grace abound toward you, that you, always having all sufficiency in all things, may have an abundance for every good work.

Just press the pause button here and once again allow the revelation of *2 Corinthians 9:8* to go even deeper into your soul than ever before.

For us the revelation was that if God is able, then whatever changes we needed to make we would commit to doing so. You, too, are not in a lost or hopeless situation; there is not some shadow over you that says you are never going to have enough or be able to experience breakthrough. 'That you, always having all sufficiency' – you and I are called to live in a place where we no longer need to have money determining any of our major life decisions. It may not happen overnight, but it will happen if we continue to walk the pathway.

## LIVING THE BALANCE
This whole teaching of *God Money & Me* is based on God's

principles for building financial freedom. How do we get the right balance? Right now, I am getting very excited and expectant about the final segment as all the foundational teaching will culminate in four practical and strategic solutions. This will change everything for us.

Almost half the parables, in fact 16 out of the 38 that Jesus taught, were around money, stewardship and material things. He understood how powerful money is and how quickly we get distracted and seduced by it.

American pastor and writer A.W. Tozer has said that 'As base a thing as money often is, yet it can be transmuted into everlasting treasure.' In other words, money is not just about the here and now: it has everlasting consequences. 'It can be converted to food for the hungry,' said Tozer, 'clothing for the poor, keep a missionary actively winning the lost to the light of the gospel. Any temporal possession can be turned into everlasting wealth. Whatever is given to Christ is immediately touched with immortality.'

In the next chapter, we will look at activating our authority in Christ when it comes to the promised blessing God has for us.

# TWENTY-THREE

# THE AUTHORITY OF THE ASK

Learning how to live in a state of freedom when it comes to money requires a blend of knowledge, understanding and wisdom. We need to live out God's principles within a spirit of unwavering expectation.

It is not mystical magic where we sit back and wait for God to work a miracle. Remember, God is wanting to position you to build a foundation for financial freedom. He wants to give evidence of His abundant favor towards you, but we must become a willing participant before we become a recipient. The following passage from James puts the situation in clear, unadorned language.

> **We must become a willing participant before we become a recipient**

*James 4:2–3* *You want what you don't have, so you scheme and kill to get it. You are jealous of what others have, but you can't get it, so you fight and wage war to take it away from them. Yet you don't have what you want because you don't ask God for it. And even when you ask, you don't get it because your motives are all wrong – you want only what will give you pleasure.* (NLT)

Absolute boldness, fueled by pure motive, is our heart attitude as we approach God to ask for what He has promised. Do you truly understand the authority we have inherited and possess as sons and daughters to come before Him with our requests?

## If you fail to ask, you fail to access

If you fail to ask, you fail to access, or if it is just for your selfish desires, you will not unlock God's unlimited provision.

We all have an active enemy who consistently works to stop us from entering in and accessing our rights as God's children.

**John 10:10** *The thief does not come except to steal, and to kill, and to destroy. I have come that they may have life, and that they may have it more abundantly.*

The activation of the ask happens when we know, with all humility, that God is sovereign over our material possessions. From the security of this, we have the right to proceed and boldly activate the ask. In other words, if our motives are genuine, we have a right to hold God to His word.

If we are going to bring freedom to our finances, we have to activate the right kind of ask – and that has three primary aspects.

## ONE – ASK WITH GOD-GIVEN AUTHORITY
All of us need to ask with God-given authority. It becomes easy for us to dilute our expectations, especially over a period of time

when we fail to see a breakthrough.

I was one of eight children. My parents did an amazing job raising us, but I remember repeatedly being told to be thankful for what we had, as there were many less fortunate than us who had nothing. The net result was that we simply didn't ask for anything outside of the expected. Even as I entered adulthood, I had to push past the feelings of being uncomfortable about asking.

Many times I felt I was not entitled to ask for anything. Now I understand things quite differently: once we have honored God, we can anticipate and expect that He will honor us. To ask for what God has promised is to activate the authority of heaven. Lack is often the outcome when authority is not present. I believe God is saying: 'I am looking for people who will activate their authority to become receivers of My promises.' Take a look at this next verse.

> Once we have honored God, we can anticipate and expect that He will honor us

*Psalm 2:7-8* *I will declare the decree: The LORD has said to Me, 'You are My Son, today I have begotten You. Ask of Me, and I will give You the nations for Your inheritance, and the ends of the earth for Your possession.*

Note he said, 'I will declare'…. If we live with uncertain expectations, or a feeling of having no right to expect good things, we limit God's ability to expand our worlds. Maybe you feel unworthy to have that level of boldness with God?

*1 John 3:21-22* *Beloved, if our heart does not condemn us, we have confidence toward God. And whatever we ask we receive from Him, because we keep His commandments and do those things that are pleasing in His sight.*

It is true that many of us accept self-condemnation too quickly and fail to stand in our God-given authority. Often it is the residue of negative words spoken over us, wrong theology, or we have succumbed to the enemy's plan for us to live a 'survival only' life.

To be able to exercise the authority of the ask, we need to be clear that God's promises are 'Yes and Amen'.

---

**We have succumbed to the enemy's plan for us to live a 'survival only' life**

---

Entrepreneur and author Jim Rohn said 'Asking is the beginning of receiving. Make sure you don't go to the ocean with a teaspoon. At least take a bucket so the kids won't laugh at you.'

## TWO – ASK WITH KINGDOM PURPOSE

We need to ask within the boundaries of kingdom purpose – if not, we are asking amiss. I am not talking about a 'Bless Me Only' club. Don't get me wrong, God wants to bless you, but the end, as we have made quite clear so far, is not simply for your pleasure. God delights to give you the desires of your heart, while at the same time activating His purposes in and through you.

In *1 Chronicles 4:9* we find the story of Jabez, who prayed to be blessed and to have his territory enlarged. God granted him his request of abundant blessing because Jabez was praying within the boundaries of kingdom purpose.

Maree and I have seen this kind of kingdom provision repeatedly. One striking example comes to mind. Many years ago, we felt God speak to us about buying a car for someone who was in need. At the time it was a rather big step but we had a deep sense it was God. We went to the bank and increased our mortgage and bought the car.

It wasn't long after that that Maree came to me and said, 'I can't get rid of this feeling that we should buy a car for my mum.' Her mum was walking through a tough season and really needed to be mobile. To be honest, I wasn't filled with the same level of grace, revelation, or whatever you would like to call it, that Maree had about what she felt we should do. I'm not too proud of the way I responded as I said to her, 'Well, if God spoke to you about it, you "Go to God"'. My human reality was we had just purchased a car for someone also in need and I couldn't see how we could afford another.

Her response was, 'Well, I will then – I'll go to God,' and she did. Talk about the activation of the ask based on what she felt God say. If you know Maree, she knows how to pray and she doesn't mince words when she has a mandate from God. It became one of those big lessons for me as I look back, where the Holy Spirit taught me a crucial element in releasing God's promised provision: the activation of the ask in alignment with God's purposes.

Here's how the miracle happened. Later that same year a pastor from the USA came to the women's conference that Maree was leading and requested to see her. Maree sat there spellbound as the woman told Maree that God had spoken to her before she left to come to the conference, telling her to buy Maree a car. She then handed over the keys to a brand-new car!

You can imagine the waterworks that ensued as the literal answer to Maree's ask manifested. That gift enabled Maree to sell her old car and buy her mother a car with the proceeds.

Maree stood in God-centered authority. She didn't say 'I hope this will work', and yet deep down thought it probably wouldn't. She stood on her ask authority in God and believed in faith, because she knew God wanted it and that her prayer would be answered. Many of us know the verses in *John 15* well.

*John 15:7-8* *If you abide in Me, and My words abide in you, you will ask what you desire, and it shall be done for you. By this My Father is glorified, that you bear much fruit; so you will be My disciples.*

Jesus taught that when you get your heart aligned, and live within the boundaries of kingdom purpose, you will ask. It is my belief that the closer you are to the heartbeat of Jesus, the more you will activate a kingdom-based ask.

Conversely, as early 20th-century evangelist Oswald Chambers has commented: 'Whenever success is made the motive of service, infidelity to our Lord is the inevitable result.'

## THREE – ASK WITH UNENDING PERSISTENCE

When it comes to asking, not only do we ask with God-given authority and with kingdom purpose but also with determined resolution concerning our requests. I believe God responds to those who have fully engaged their faith in their petitioning. Once we have presented our request, the challenge lies between our request and the outcome. This is the very point where the enemy seeks to sow seeds of doubt and create double-mindedness. We must decide to never give up.

Maree tells the story of a woman she met at her women's conference *Sistas*, who came up for prayer. For seven years this lady had been praying to fall pregnant, and yet she remained childless. At the conference that morning, the worship team sang the song *God is Good All The Time*. She stood there in the meeting thinking 'Well, God, I know you are good but I'm not sure if I believe you are good all the time,' and she momentarily felt reluctant to join in. However, over the course of the conference, as she felt the encouragement of the Holy Spirit, she decided she would not give in to doubt. She told Maree that during conference her heart began to believe again and she decided to put aside the seven years of disappointment that each month brought.

Activate the ask with a God-centered authority, wrapped in unwavering persistence

A year later she returned to *Sistas* with a little baby in her arms. She recounted how she had in that moment of worship said to herself, 'I take my position as a daughter of God' and she activated the ask with a God-centered authority, wrapped in unwavering persistence.

We find in *Luke 11* the story of the man who kept pestering his friend for a loaf of bread at midnight because he had received an unexpected visitor. Jesus explains to the disciples that the man wouldn't respond to the request because of the lateness of the hour, but finally said yes 'because of his friend's persistence'. Then Jesus went on to say:

**Luke 11:9-10** *So I say to you, ask, and it will be given to you; seek, and you will find; knock, and it will be opened to you. For everyone who asks receives, and he who seeks finds, and to him who knocks it will be opened.*

This is far more than a throwaway line: it contains an embedded truth – to ask we must verbalize an area of need; we must then seek for it like hidden treasure, and knock long enough to awaken the supplier to respond.

If we are going to release a breakthrough in our finances, we have to actually arise and say 'I am going to stand in my God-given authority and say this is my right.' Our marriages, our families, our businesses will see the blessing of God and this is our inheritance as His children.

Remember, if God has called you to it, remind yourself that you will not give in, nor will you give up. You may have suffered many failures, and currently find yourself overcome by money issues, but remember, it is not over yet. To use a sports analogy, if you are going to be part of a winning team, follow these three key rules:

- Don't look at the scoreboard;
- Keep to the game plan; and
- Commit 100 percent until the final whistle.

## PERSISTENCE UNDERSTANDS IT IS NOT OVER YET!

Here is a thought: 'Prayer protects the connection between God and man.'

There was a widow woman in *Luke 18* who, through her persistence, got an unjust judge to eventually help her, even though he refused at first. What is so amazing about this story is that Jesus used it to describe how our heavenly Father responds to us.

### Prayer protects the connection between God and man

*Luke 18:3-8 Now there was a widow in that city; and she came to him, saying, 'Get justice for me from my adversary.' And he would not for a while; but afterward he said within himself, 'Though I do not fear God nor regard man, yet because this widow troubles me I will avenge her, lest by her continual coming she weary me.' Then the Lord said, 'Hear what the unjust judge said. And shall God not avenge His own elect who cry out day and night to Him, though He bears long with them? I tell you that He will avenge them speedily. Nevertheless, when the Son of Man comes, will He really find faith on the earth?'*

I find it mind-blowing that we all give up too easily. My prayer is that once you complete *God Money & Me*, you will embrace the principles and then keep at it until God's promised breakthrough comes.

Remember, it took over 100 years for Noah to build the ark without a sign of rain and yet he lived by the promise and the purpose of God. I think we are thankful he did, or we would not be here. The same is true for the generations that follow us. If we get our material world sorted out, it will be in a very different position to release God's purposes than the one we find ourselves in today.

Someone once said that persistence is like wrestling a gorilla. You don't give up when you get tired; you give up when the gorilla gets tired!

Consistent prayer can be a bit like that! As the famous French chemist and microbiologist Louis Pasteur, the man who today is regarded as one of the founders of germ theory, said, 'Let me tell you the secret that has led me to my goal: my strength lies solely in my tenacity.'

Our next chapter will take a close look at the four levels of giving we are called to aspire to, from the not-wrong-but-limited basic level of giving out of self-interest to the highest level: a ministry of giving that responds to supernatural revelation.

# TWENTY-FOUR

# THE FOUR LEVELS
# OF GIVING

As a boy, I had a dream of giving millions away – I really did. If I hadn't gone into full-time Church work, I would have gone into business with a desire to give millions of dollars away… Now I am consumed by this thought – wouldn't it be wonderful if God's Church could be in a position to give millions away?

There has never been a better time for the Church to step up and produce a generation who could influence our cities and our society by becoming the answer to need – to become, as prophesied in *Deuteronomy 28:13*, 'the head and not the tail'.

The truth is we are all too often taught two extremes when it comes to the way we regard material wealth. Neither of them accurately reflects what the *Bible* teaches. On the one hand, we've promoted the mistruth that poverty is the path to true holiness. Some have coupled righteousness with poverty, suggesting that the more righteous you become the less you will have. The other extreme is the propagation of a self-based prosperity that claims that God wants you to have more of what you want, instead of stating the truth that God provides abundantly so you can be blessed and be a channel of blessing to others.

## We are called to live with righteousness and wealth

It's a surprise for some believers to be confronted with the idea that we are called to live with righteousness and wealth.

*Psalm 35:27 Let them shout for joy and be glad, who favor my righteous cause. And let them say continually, 'Let the LORD be magnified, who has pleasure in the prosperity of His servant.'*

## MISGUIDED AND VOID OF AN ANSWER

If you are one of those who believed it was holy to claim 'I'm not into financial abundance' – or you have thought, 'I'm quite happy with what I've got, thank you very much' – then I'd like to suggest that you are living far below biblical truth. God's purposes are so much more than just about you. How selfish is it to be only concerned about your own position? Remember, as we have seen, if God can't trust you with money, why would He release true riches? Money is our testing ground.

British wartime Prime Minister Sir Winston Churchill said: 'We make a living by what we get. We make a life by what we give.'

The truth is that we need a rather large paradigm shift in our thinking when it comes to giving, lest we fall into the trap of taking all the credit for our prosperity. Way back in *Deuteronomy* the Israelites were warned about the dangers of this kind of self-satisfaction.

*Deuteronomy 8:17-18 If you start thinking to yourselves, 'I did all this. And all by myself. I'm rich. It's all mine!' – well, think again. Remember that* GOD, *your God, gave you the strength to produce all this wealth so as to confirm the covenant that He promised to your ancestors – as it is today.* (MSG)

The facts are that the global purposes of God right now are being limited because of a lack of finance. If there were more release of finance, there would be a greater demonstration of God at work in our cities and towns. God wants to turn us into wildly generous and caring people, who mirror a wildly caring and generous God.

Gun Denhart, the founder of the Hanna Andersson clothing company, based in Portland, Oregon, has said: 'Money is like manure. If you let it pile up, it just smells. But if you spread it around, you can encourage things to grow.'

## Giving is a fundamental aspect of God's economy

It is so important we grasp the importance of giving, because if we fail to do so, we will also limit the release we expect. Giving is a fundamental aspect of God's economy.

## LEVEL ONE – SELF-INTEREST

There are four levels of giving we can aspire to, beginning with the most basic one – motivated by self-interest. When we operate at this level of giving, we give because we understand that if we sow seed, we will reap a harvest. Reward is our motive, as we understand the active and God-designed principle of sowing and reaping. It is not wrong to operate at this level but it is the lowest of the four levels.

*Luke 6:38* would reflect this position fairly accurately, when it states: 'Give, and it will be given to you: good measure, pressed down, shaken together, and running over will be put into your bosom. **For with the same measure that you use, it will be**

**measured back to you.'**

## LEVEL TWO – SPIRITUAL GRATITUDE

This is where our giving is based on understanding what God has given us. We bless because we have been blessed. The depth of our appreciation is what creates the foundation to this second response. Obligation is not the reason. Rather, we want to say thank you and partner in seeing others also experience all that God has done for us. We know we can't ever pay God back and He is not looking for that, but we want to emulate His generosity with a depth of gratitude.

The apostle Paul urges the New Testament believers to value the cost behind salvation.

*1 Corinthians 6:19-20 Or do you not know that your body is the temple of the Holy Spirit who is in you, whom you have from God, and you are not your own? For you were bought at a price; therefore glorify God in your body and in your spirit, which are God's.*

My salvation cost God everything in Jesus and now I am not my own; I am all about the purposes of my Master. Once we really understand what God has done for us through the death and resurrection of Jesus, we too realize how frail we are without Him. I think the psalmist understood this:

*Psalm 8:1-6 O LORD, our Lord, how excellent is Your name in all the earth, who have set Your glory above the heavens! Out of the mouth of babes and nursing infants You have ordained strength, because of Your enemies, that You may silence the enemy and the avenger. When I consider Your heavens, the work of Your fingers, the moon and the stars, which You have ordained, what is man that You are mindful of him, and the son of man that You visit him? For You have made him a little lower than the angels, and You have crowned him with glory and honor. You have made him to have dominion over the works of Your hands; You have put all things under his feet.*

## LEVEL THREE – SELFLESS OBEDIENCE

The more mature we become and the greater our revelation of abiding in Jesus is, the easier it is simply to obey. The matters of trust have been settled because we know Him and we decide to trust that God's word works.

> Decide to trust that God's word works

This does not mean that levels one and two are no longer relevant, but now our soul has become increasingly subject to our spirit man and we commit to live the word of God. For some of us, the reality of our current world can restrict the formation of the right God-centered pathway.

Can I encourage you to consider God's word, which is truth, and determine to live life when it comes to giving according to His patterns and principles in the area of money, which will create a pathway to financial freedom.

**Psalm 40:8** *I delight to do Your will, O my God, and Your law is within my heart.*

## LEVEL FOUR – SUPERNATURAL REVELATION

I believe this is the highest form of giving. Ultimately each one of us are to live out the revelations we possess. Years ago at LIFE, we made a decision that we would no longer take up offerings during the service, but provide containers at the doors and giving stations in the foyer. The reason behind this was that I believe if we teach truth and people live out of the revelation of God's word, breakthrough takes place. This fourth level of giving is because we no longer need weekly convincing – we simply believe and activate God's word.

When you live a revelation, you experience the freedom that comes with it

It is amazing what happens when you say 'YES' and are obedient to God's word. When you live a revelation, you experience the freedom that comes with it.

*Isaiah 32:8 But a generous man devises generous things, and by generosity he shall stand.*

The reality for all of us is that we will ultimately live out the revelations we carry. My prayer, once again, is that the Holy Spirit will reveal to you the truth of God's word when it comes to your financial world, which, once mixed with obedience, creates a pathway to financial freedom.

I love this quote by pastor and author Brennan Manning: 'The greatest cause of atheism is Christians who acknowledge Jesus with their lips, then walk out the door and deny Him with their lifestyle. That is what an unbelieving world finds simply unbelievable.' That is something for all who profess a Christian faith to consider.

In our final part, Part Five, I am going to introduce the **'10/10/10/80 PRINCIPLE'**, which will give you the four key ingredients to creating a future of financial freedom. A pathway that, once embraced, will unlock the complete promises of God in your financial and material worlds and go on to create a platform for generational blessing.

# MONEY'S RELEASE

---

Once we have honored God first, we have a God-given right to ask Him for an abundance for every good work. Once our hearts are aligned, we are positioned to see a breakthrough as God has promised to bless. Remember: God amplifies the aligned. Our challenge now is to live beyond small-mindedness and expect God's favor in our material world.

We have all been chosen to become a human channel of provision by a loving and all-able God. If we fail to believe that, we limit not only ourselves, but also the purposes of God in helping others through us.

## MAIN REFLECTION POINTS:

1. Have you found it difficult to believe God for financial break-through? If so, why?

_____

_____

_____

_____

_____

_____

_____


2. *James* teaches us that we have not because we ask not. Write out *James 4:2-3*. What would be an experience from your past that would limit you from asking (placing an expectation on God)?

_____

_____

_____

_____

_____

_____


3. Persistence in our believing God to fulfill His promises seems to be so important *(Luke 18:3-8)*. Why do you think that is the case?

_____

_____

4. Of the four levels of giving listed in Chapter 24, which one do you usually give out of and why?

5. Write out the prayer of Jabez found in *1 Chronicles 4:9-10.* Why do you think God granted him his request?

6. Explain why a farmer who sows his/her seed would expect a harvest.

7. What is the main thing you have got out of Part Four of *God Money & Me*?

# PART FIVE
# MONEY'S PATHWAY

# TWENTY-FIVE

# FOUR INGREDIENTS TO CREATING A FINANCIAL FUTURE

W e've come to the final section of *God Money & Me* where, on the basis of everything that has gone before, I will outline the four ingredients that, when working together, will literally change everything about our future finances. This is where 'the rubber really hits the road' as we choose to decide whether to implement the needed change or simply nod our heads in approval.

In this chapter, I want to focus on what is necessary to create a sound financial future, both in our everyday finances and for future generations.

## INGREDIENT ONE – **STEWARDING**
Being a good steward of the resources we've received begins with being intentional in how we facilitate and deploy our increase, whether large or small. Kiwi entrepreneur Robert Laidlaw, who built the Farmers Trading Company, a large New Zealand retail business, was clear on the importance of sound stewardship of his

finances. Speaking towards the end of his life, he said: 'In spiritual communion and in material things, God has blessed me one hundred-fold, and has graciously entrusted to me a stewardship far beyond my expectations when, as a lad of 18, I started to give God a definite portion of my wages.'

To be a good and faithful steward of something means to preserve and maintain, safeguard and protect, and generally take care of what has been entrusted to us. Our responsibility is to ensure it is used wisely and releases God's intended purposes. As we have seen in a biblical context, the first priority God places on good stewarding of our finances is to return what belongs to Him, by tithing the first tenth of our increase into the storehouse. We have described this in Part Three as 'resetting sovereignty' over our money so that God, El Shaddai, remains ascendant over all of our financial resources. We'll come back to this again in Chapter 26.

### INGREDIENT TWO – SEEDING

Seeding is the revelation of God's principle of 'seedtime and harvest'. Like many in the Church, I've been taught soundly on the need to tithe, but in my earlier years, I never heard it said that tithing and giving seed were different. 'Seeding' applies to any area where we sow resources, time and talents beyond ourselves. Simply put, God makes it clear that our harvest is ultimately the result of the seed we sow. We will devote Chapters 27 and 28 to explaining in more detail about the concept of seedtime and harvest, as it is a critical part of the full plan.

> **Our harvest is ultimately the result of the seed we sow**

### INGREDIENT THREE – SAVING

Our understanding of the meaning of 'saving' is that it is a long-term investment that primarily ends up as a financial foundation for future generations. This is also where we create an answer to current debt, and unlock the ability to bless our children and our children's children. Ultimately, our aim would be to match our saving with our seeding. We will explore this a little further in Chapter 29.

**Proverbs 21:5** *The plans of the diligent lead surely to plenty, but those of everyone who is hasty, surely to poverty.*

## INGREDIENT FOUR – SPENDING
This is possibly the area where the majority of us have the most experience, but often attach the least wisdom to. As you can imagine, there is a big difference between what we should be doing and what we are doing. Our spending must be in line with pre-established boundaries if we are to create a pathway to financial freedom. Chapter 30 will discuss this challenging area in more detail.

## FROM PRINCIPLE TO PRACTICE
Looking at our finances as a mixture of these four ingredients – stewarding, seeding, saving and spending – may initially appear overly simplistic, but when combined and implemented with a right understanding, these four areas become the pathway to financial release.

> There will be many temptations to compromise along the way

We would be naive not to assume that there will be many temptations to compromise along the way. However, this blend of stewarding, seeding, saving and spending is what I believe is at the core of our personal financial breakthrough. We'll look at how these four ingredients work together in Chapter 31.

## WISDOM'S FRUIT

We are constantly reminded in *Proverbs* that an effective kingdom life requires the application of continual wisdom. In *Proverbs 8:17*, Wisdom says it 'loves those who love her'.

> ## We can't afford just to 'park' and be satisfied with what we know

In other words, we can't afford just to 'park' and be satisfied with what we know, but must pursue wisdom continually. Wisdom goes on to say: 'Those who seek me diligently will find me.' We can be assured that God has ALL the wisdom we need to live by.

***Proverbs 8:18*** *Riches and honor are with me, enduring riches and righteousness.*

It's amazing to me how many scriptures, both in the Old and the New Testaments, put the righteousness of God in a context with financial blessing. There is something important about this dialogue and this cohabitation of money and true riches that we shouldn't overlook. According to *Proverbs 8:21*, those who love wisdom will inherit wealth and have full treasuries.

Let's now focus on the first of these four keys to creating a pathway to financial freedom – stewarding.

# TWENTY-SIX

# 'STEWARDING' – RETURN WHAT BELONGS TO GOD

---

In Part Three – Money's Test, we looked at how the tithe or first tenth of all our increase, once returned, honors God. As this is an important and often challenging concept, let's take a moment to review how tithing enables us to reject the spirit of mammon and reset God's sovereignty over our material world.

## TITHING – THE FOUNDATIONAL SCRIPTURE

The Old Testament prophet Malachi, writing in *Malachi 3*, gives us a foundational scripture to help us understand the tithing principle. And, once again, before you say, 'That's Old Testament,' let's think it through. Yes, it is true – we do not live under the law. However, the Old Testament is filled with truth that transforms. Do we believe in the Ten Commandments? That's Old Testament. If you think the Old Testament is completely irrelevant, then there would be no purpose for it to exist today, apart from as a historical reminder.

Although Jesus came and fulfilled the Old Testament law and

brought into play a new covenant, the Old Testament remains God's word and is far from irrelevant, as we will see.

*Malachi 3:6-10* *'For I am the Lord, I do not change; Therefore you are not consumed, O sons of Jacob. Yet from the days of your fathers you have gone away from My ordinances and have not kept them. Return to Me, and I will return to you,' says the Lord of hosts. 'But you said, "In what way shall we return?" Will a man rob God? Yet you have robbed Me! But you say, "In what way have we robbed You?" In tithes and offerings. You are cursed with a curse, for you have robbed Me, even this whole nation. Bring all the tithes into the storehouse, that there may be food in My house, and try Me now in this,' says the Lord of hosts, 'If I will not open for you the windows of heaven and pour out for you such blessing that there will not be room enough to receive it.'*

Firstly, note the tone and the tense. 'For I am the Lord, I do not change; Therefore you are not consumed, O sons of Jacob. Yet from the days of your fathers you have gone away from My ordinances.'

## For I am the Lord, I do not change

God begins by making reference to Himself and how His people had drifted away from Him and His ordinances. This was and is far more than an Old Testament law. Note He said: 'I do not change...'

God was saying: 'This is about Me and who I am, not just about what I want you to do.' Allow me to paraphrase it further: 'I am God and I never change and yet you have turned away from Me, My laws, My ordinances, My statutes, My way of living and from Me. These are the patterns, the structures that will release My authority over you. Yet you have gone away from them and you have not kept them.'

Note what God asks: 'Would you return to Me?' Not just: 'Would you do what I ask – tick all the right boxes and simply fulfill My laws?' But: 'Would you return to Me?' This is very personal. He goes on: 'If you return to Me, then I will return to you. If you allow Me to be sovereign, then I will draw you into My proximity. But you said "In which way would we return to You?"'

## The tithe or the first tenth of all our increase does not belong to us but to God

The very next thing God says is: 'Will a man rob God? ... You say "In what way have we robbed you?"' God responds with: 'In tithes and offerings.' The tithe or the first tenth of all our increase does not belong to us but to God. Note that God separates the tithe and the offerings, as they are very different. It is true that the tithe or the first tenth was required during the time of the Old Testament law, but it was also offered before the law was established, and Jesus took time in *Matthew* to say we should continue it within the New Testament.

So, tithing is:
* in the Old Testament *(Leviticus 27:30-32)*
* activated before the law *(Genesis 14:18-20)*
* required after the law *(Matthew 23:23)*.

## FIVE COMMON QUESTIONS ABOUT TITHING

### ONE – 'DO I TITHE ON MY GROSS INCOME OR ON THE NET?'

After years of thinking this through, and deliberating with many people, I'd say it depends on what, or whom, you put first. So, is it God first or taxes first?

If you choose to tithe on the net (income after tax), what you are effectively saying is that you don't consider that you personally benefit from anything your tax dollars are spent on. The truth is, the tax that we all pay provides the infrastructure and many other advantages we rely on in the country of our residence.

Let's look at what the *Bible* says. *Mark 12* tells us that the Pharisees plotted how they might entangle Jesus with their questions. They said to Him:

**Mark 12:14** *Teacher, we know that You are true, and care about no one; for You do not regard the person of men, but teach the way of God in truth.*

The Pharisees approached Jesus with a deceptive agenda in order to try and trip Him up. They continued: 'Is it lawful to pay taxes to Caesar, or not? Shall we pay, or shall we not pay?' Jesus perceived their wickedness and said (paraphrased): 'Why do you test Me, you hypocrites? Show Me the tax money.' So they brought Him a denarius. He said to them: 'Whose image and inscription is on this coin?' They said: 'Caesar's.' Look at Jesus's response.

**Mark 12:17** *And Jesus answered and said to them, 'Render to Caesar the things that are Caesar's, and to God the things that are God's.' And they marveled at Him.*

Let me just throw this in: even if you don't like the tax laws, or don't think you benefit much from how tax dollars are spent, God says we are to honor them. If you don't want to pay the tax, I suppose the only answer is: don't live in the country. Ultimately, Christians should respect and embrace the laws under which they live, unless they violate God's word. It's a matter of authority. I believe Jesus taught we were to put God first in everything and then give honor where honor is due.

If you feel like this is a huge jump for you, remember that God said to test Him in this and you will see Him open the windows of heaven and pour out a blessing. Right now is where we start to realize that the pathway to financial freedom will require our obedience and trust. God's tithe is our test. Our tithe has never really been ours to choose whether to bring it or not. In God's eyes, it has never been optional.

---

### God's tithe is our test

---

We'll return to the questions of how we should be using our income before and after tax – and how each of the four ingredients work together – in Chapter 31.

### TWO – 'WHAT IF I CAN'T AFFORD TO TITHE?'

This is a big one, because we've all been there. In *1 Kings 17*, Elijah comes to the widow at Zarephath. She and her son are facing impending death as she only has a little bit of oil and flour left. As a family, they are about to eat their last meal before starving. Elijah, who represents God's authority, arrives on the scene just when everything seems lost. The widow calls in a panic-stricken way to Elijah, telling him, 'We're going to die.' His response in the first instance seems the opposite of what we would expect from a man of God. Instead of finding supplies for her, he says, 'Bring to me what you have.'

I believe this story has a lot to teach us. Elijah understood the power of 'the first' and what is released when God is honored. The widow responded with complete trust by making a meal for the man of God first. In other words, her prioritizing of God in first place brought about miraculous provision.

*1 Kings 17:15-16 So she went away and did according to the word of Elijah; and she and he and her household ate for many days. The bin of flour was not used up, nor did the jar of oil run dry, according to the word of the Lord which He spoke by Elijah.*

We are all constantly confronted by our natural limitations and current realities, but God's way works. Remember, it's God who gave us life and breath, who put the sun in the sky to give us warmth. He created our world, which not only provides for our needs but also fulfills our desires. When we find ourselves at our lowest point, the wisest thing we can do is to place Jesus in a position of authority over our lack of resources. In all seriousness, we can't afford NOT to tithe (that is, position God first in our finances), whether we find ourselves with an absence or abundance of funds.

## THREE – 'WHAT CONSTITUTES MY INCREASE?'

If I'm to tithe, to put God first and honor Him in my increase, I need to answer one important question: what constitutes my increase? Once again, this may sound too simple, but increase is increase. Whenever you expand or advance in any monetary way, the first tenth is God's.

So, if you're on a salary, it's pretty easy: whatever you get in your salary, the first tenth goes to God. However, many Christians have not considered other places where they may also experience increase. For example, if you buy a house and sell it, the difference between your purchase price and the sale price is your profit; you tithe on that.

> Tithing is not the paying of a bill but a decision of lordship

Anytime we receive any form of personal benefit, it equals increase. Therefore, our salary, a return on investments, inheritances, capital increase, monetary gifts – these are all forms of increase where we are to honor God. The reason we do this is that every time you experience financial increase, your choice to tithe wards off the attachment of mammon. Tithing is not the paying of a bill but a decision of lordship. As I look back over my own life, as far back as I can remember, I have never not honored God with the first tenth of my increase. It is amazing, however, that at times it is still a decision that I have to choose to make.

Often, business people ask:'How do we tithe if we are in business?' For those in a start-up business, whatever you pay yourself is your increase. If you own a business, you could assess the value of your business annually and tithe on what you personally take out. Or, when you sell the business, look at what its value is then. Whatever you have seen the business increase in value by is your increase.

## FOUR – 'IS IT OK TO TITHE TO OTHER MINISTRIES?'

There are many great ministries that deserve support, but where the tithe goes is not ours to decide. It is God's, and we are called to return it to God and place it where He has chosen it to go.

> It is not my tithe but His tithe

My understanding is that in *Malachi 3:10*, where it says: 'Bring all the tithes into the storehouse', God's ultimate plan is to see the tithe come into His house, as He has purposed the Church to become the cornerstone of society.

Remember, it is not my tithe but His, and God says it belongs in the storehouse. Seed is to be differentiated from the tithe. When it comes to other ministries, missionaries and needs, those are things into which we can sow seed, and we have the rest of our disposable income available to us for that purpose. It is out of what remains *after* the tithe that we can decide what we will use as seed. *Exodus 23* makes it very clear:

**Exodus 23:19** *The first of the first fruits of your land you shall bring into the house of the Lord your God.*

According to *Exodus 23*, the storehouse – that is, the Church – is where our tithe belongs. Everything after God's tithe is under our direction and discretion. I know this can be challenging for some, but if we set this in order, the Church will become resourced to function fully, in line with God's plan.

We will discover more about how seeding works with the other elements in our financial pathway in Chapters 27 and 31.

## FIVE – 'DOES MY TITHING GUARANTEE FINANCIAL BREAKTHROUGH?'

You might be surprised at this, but I would have to say 'no'. Being faithful to return God's tithe is the foundation and beginning point – it releases God's blessing over the rest of my income. Once we have denied the spirit of mammon access, we also release God's promised protection and provision.

> When I tithe, God enters into partnership with my financial world

However, I am still responsible to make the right choices over the balance of all my increase. When I tithe, God enters into partnership with my financial world, but I need His wisdom attached to my remaining resources.

This was where so much began to change for me. While I had always understood the part about securing lordship and sovereignty over my finances, I didn't understand what else was needed to complete the picture of a pathway to financial freedom. Along with stewarding (returning what belongs to God), a correct understanding of seeding, saving and spending is also vital. I was never taught this in Church, but I realize now that once we merge all four elements into a comprehensive financial practice, everything ties together to release God's blessing and liberate us to experience financial freedom.

We'll come back to that in Chapter 31, but for now, let's take a look at the second in our four ingredients to establishing a financial pathway – seeding.

# TWENTY-SEVEN

# 'SEEDING' – CREATING THE HARVEST

The second strand in the cord that connects us to God's answer to living a financial breakthrough is activating the law of seedtime and harvest. The realization that tithing alone is not enough answers a lot of questions as to why we still experience lack after honoring God with the first tenth. To create the right financial foundation, more than one ingredient is required.

## THE FIRST INGREDIENT – GOD AMPLIFIES WHAT IS ALIGNED

We are aligned if we are following the principles of firstfruits and tithing (stewarding), which we discussed in Chapter 22 and Chapter 26 just now.

## THE SECOND INGREDIENT – THE MOVE FROM 'NEED' TO 'SEED CONSCIOUSNESS'

On my journey to discover an answer to our personal lack, I discovered that tithing, which positioned God as sovereign, was only the beginning of a number of adjustments that needed to happen. After rereading *Malachi 3*, I saw that not only was Israel robbing God by not tithing, but was also robbing Him through its lack of offerings – seeding.

***Malachi 3:6–8*** *'For I am the Lord, I do not change; Therefore you are not consumed, O sons of Jacob. Yet from the days of your fathers you have gone away from My ordinances and have not kept them. Return to Me, and I will return to you,' says the Lord of hosts. 'But you said, "In what way shall we return?" Will a man rob God? Yet you have robbed Me!* ***But you say, "In what way have we robbed You?" In tithes and offerings.'*** [emphasis added]

This hit me like a bolt of lightning, as I realized that positioning God first with the tithe was one thing, and sowing seed was another. I'm not sure if you have ever thought about this, but to tithe is not sowing seed. While tithing is returning what doesn't belong to you, seeding opens the door to harvest.

I think much of the body of Christ is yet to appreciate the difference between stewarding (tithing) and seeding. I mentioned previously how Maree and I embarked on a seeding journey that led us to giving away 37 percent of our gross income. What a joy it was

> Move from a 'need' consciousness to a 'seed' consciousness

and yet challenging at the same time. We decided to move from a 'need' consciousness to a 'seed' consciousness.

## THE LAW OF SEEDTIME AND HARVEST
Genesis shows us that the day that Adam and Eve sinned, the ground became cursed. It remained cursed until the time of Noah. Simply put, it was almost impossible to put seed in the ground and get a full harvest. The only way you could do it was by the toil and the sweat of your brow. Today, that curse has been

lifted. Of course, there are still weeds, but nothing like the time between the Fall and Noah. Any one of us can plant a carrot seed and get carrots. We fail to realize that the curse was broken when Noah, after the flood, offered a sweet-smelling aroma in *Genesis 8*.

*Genesis 8:20-21* *Then Noah built an altar to the Lord, and took of every clean animal and of every clean bird, and offered burnt offerings on the altar. And the Lord smelled a soothing aroma. Then the Lord said in His heart, 'I will never again curse the ground for man's sake, although the imagination of man's heart is evil from his youth; nor will I again destroy every living thing as I have done.'*

When God said that He would 'never again curse the ground for man's sake, and … never again destroy the earth because you've done this thing' (paraphrased), He instituted a law that still operates today – the law of seedtime and harvest:

*Genesis 8:22* *While the earth remains, seedtime and harvest, cold and heat, winter and summer, and day and night shall not cease.*

This verse carries such profound truth that, once realized, will release blessing in and through our lives. It is an immutable, unstoppable law that will remain as long as the earth remains. There will be seedtime and harvest, cold and heat, summer and winter, day and night. It is interesting that you and I have control over only one of those four things, and that is the law of seedtime and harvest. Day and night, cold and heat, summer and winter – all of these will continue to happen. But each of us gets to determine the harvest by sowing seed, giving it time and reaping the reward. We must all come to realize that many things are beyond our control, but the harvest is not one of them.

> Many things are beyond our control, but the harvest is not one of them

There is a lot of debate about money in the Church, but there seems to be little debate about the fact that seed produces harvest. Once we understand that seedtime and harvest form a divine law, much like the way gravity is a law, we all can activate a greater harvest through our seed.

Think about the law of gravity: it keeps you grounded here on earth and prevents you from drifting around the universe. You are bound by it, and you cannot deny that it exists. But, if you try, you can defy it or prevent it from working effectively. If I was to jump off a chair, I would fall down because of gravity. However, I can defy gravity by engaging another law called the law of thrust. If I board an airplane, by the law of thrust I defy gravitational law. On the other hand, if the plane's engine fails, I will come back under the established divine law of gravity.

## God responds to our response

In the same way, the law of seedtime and harvest is an irrefutable law; it's the way that life operates. The issue is not that we deny the existence of the seedtime and harvest law, it's the fact that we fail to activate sowing seed and, as a result, we are not releasing our promised harvest. In other words, God responds to our response. God is looking for people who will honor Him with the first and then also instigate the law of seedtime and harvest.

## CHOCOLATE ECLAIR TIME

I was a pastry cook for four years, as my mom and dad were involved in the food industry and I worked for them in their business. One of the things I still love to cook are chocolate eclairs. I am amazed by how many people love them, and people are often surprised when they discover that I can actually make them. The fact is, to make the eclair casings, you need only four ingredients: butter, water, flour and salt. One of the keys to great eclairs is to have the mixture still warm when you pipe them onto the tray, and then place them into a hot and steamy oven that remains closed until they are ready.

All going well, you see the miracle of them rising right before your eyes. However, if you are tempted to open the oven to check them before they are ready, they will immediately fall flat.

I know this is not meant to be a cookbook, but the point I am making is that, if you don't have both the right ingredients and the right application, the recipe will fail. If you have the correct ingredients but are not employing right methods, even something as simple as eclairs will get the better of you. And that is how it is with the law of seedtime and harvest. God actually says that every one of us can successfully unlock this law of creating harvest in every area of our lives.

**Galatians 6:7** *Do not be deceived, God is not mocked; for whatever a man sows, that he will also reap.*

In the J.B. Phillips translation of the *Bible*, this reads as: 'Don't be under any illusion: you cannot make a fool of God! A man's harvest in life will depend entirely on what he sows.' (PHILLIPS)

> We can all influence the outcome of our lives by sowing seed for the harvest we want to see

In other words, if your life isn't living up to your expectations, stop blaming your situation on your past, your parents, world economics, and everyone else in your life. Take a look at what seed you are sowing. We can all influence the outcome of our lives by sowing seed for the harvest we want to see.

**2 Corinthians 9:6** *He who sows sparingly will also reap sparingly, and* *he who sows bountifully will also reap bountifully.*

The law of seedtime and harvest operates in every part of our lives. Over the years, I have had many people ask me why God is not giving them a promotion where they work. I often begin by asking this question: 'Are you the first to be there and last to leave – do you work harder than others around you?' If you expect to 'reap a harvest' at work, then sow the right 'work seeds'. If we want change in any area of our lives, the first thing we need to do is take a look at what we are sowing into it.

**2 Corinthians 9:8** *And God is able to bless you abundantly, so that in all things at all times, having all that you need, you will abound in every good work.* (NIV)

It is a challenge we all need to face up to. Remember our seed is the second ingredient in seeing *2 Corinthians 9:8* become a reality in our lives.

## GOD RESPONDS TO OUR RESPONSE

There is no doubt that the enemy wants to limit you, make you feel trapped and make you believe that change is impossible.

**2 Corinthians 9:7** *Each of you should give what you have decided in your heart to give, not reluctantly or under compulsion, for God loves a cheerful giver.* (NIV)

If you read *2 Corinthians 9* carefully – and spend some time meditating and studying this chapter – you will discover that the apostle Paul is saying that harvest requires seed.

Understanding the law of seedtime and harvest as a personal revelation is so important for our long-term financial breakthrough. We will look at this further in the next chapter, where we will talk about the different sorts of seeds we should sow and the optimum environment for producing an abundant harvest. When you fully understand this law that is at our disposal, you will become increasingly excited and faith-filled.

## TWENTY-EIGHT

# SECRETS TO SUCCESSFUL SOWING

---

D o you find sometimes that there is an unwanted voice inside your head, speaking negative messages such as 'I couldn't do that...', 'It's unfair...', 'You can't expect that...', 'It will never happen for me...'?

It's all too easy to allow wrong mind-sets developed through childhood or negative life experiences to box us into leading limited lives. We can easily find ourselves in a rut that produces a default negative response to any suggestion of expansion. As soon as we think 'I can't', we've already sown a seed that has a harvest attached to it.

> As soon as we think 'I can't', we've already sown a seed that has a harvest attached to it

**Proverbs 23:7** *For as he thinks in his heart, so is he.*

Many of us will have grown up with the feeling of being 'different' – I know I did. Just one small thing can make us feel like outsiders, especially when we are young and at school. For me, one such thing was my mom's haircuts. As I've already explained, I was one of eight children. Our family budget didn't stretch to fancy haircuts. Every so often, Mom would announce it was 'haircut time'. She would produce a bowl from the kitchen cupboard, place it over our heads, and cut around it. I felt extremely self-conscious about the result! I remember the humiliation of going to school, where I was already labeled for being a weird Christian. Now I was a weird Christian with a really bad haircut.

> Seeds of negative thoughts will fail to produce any kind of positive future gain

Simply put, seeds of negative thoughts – whether sown by us or others – will fail to produce any kind of positive future gain. Our thoughts, our words, our attitudes, our actions – and even our inaction – are all seeds that produce a harvest, whether we realize it or not.

## SOWING THE RIGHT SEEDS

Have you realized that your words create reality? *Genesis 1:3* tells us that when God was creating the universe, 'He spoke'. And as His creatures, made in His image, our words also have creative power – for good or for harm.

**Proverbs 18:21** *Death and life are in the power of the tongue.*

As soon as we say something, we are creating something – we are activating a harvest. We can't be negative and expect a positive outcome. The outcomes we see are a reflection of the source from which they spring. If we want a bountiful harvest, we have to align ourselves with God's word and start responding to the things of God. Take a look at *Hebrews 4*:

*Hebrews 4:12 For the word of God is alive and active. Sharper than any double-edged sword, it penetrates even to dividing soul and spirit, joints and marrow; it judges the thoughts and attitudes of the heart.* (NIV)

Every action and corresponding inaction are sown seeds. Many of us never use this law to our advantage because we don't value or use whatever little seed we have. The truth is that planted seeds reproduce a harvest containing more seeds.

*2 Corinthians 9:10-11 Now He who supplies seed to the sower and bread for food will also supply and increase your store of seed and will enlarge the harvest of your righteousness. You will be enriched in every way so that you can be generous on every occasion, and through us your generosity will result in thanksgiving to God.* (NIV)

God's word says He will release seed to the sower. Become a sower with intent and you will never be short of seed. Remember, seed translates to an increasing harvest. Too often we say, 'Well, I will get around to sowing when I get the seed.' But God says that's not the way it works: the commitment to become a sower comes before the realization of seed. God supplies seed to the hand that commits to sow, because such a person understands the authority of this divine law.

You don't start sowing once you have satisfied yourself that you can do it. You sow to release God's promised blessing of seeds, which contain a harvest. A harvest won't come from an inactive spirit or a mind-set of poverty.

> A harvest won't come from an inactive spirit or a mind-set of poverty

*Proverbs 13:4 The soul of a lazy man desires, and has nothing; But the soul of the diligent shall be made rich.*

## SEEDS PRODUCE AFTER THEIR OWN KIND

There are many simple but profound principles around the whole practice of seedtime and harvest that are worth securing into our spirits.

*Genesis 1:11-12* *Then God said, 'Let the earth bring forth grass, the herb that yields seed, and the fruit tree that yields fruit according to its kind, whose seed is in itself, on the earth'; and it was so. And the earth brought forth grass, the herb that yields seed according to its kind, and the tree that yields fruit, whose seed is in itself according to its kind. And God saw that it was good.*

Imagine a farmer expecting that he or she would harvest something different from what had been sown. Do you think a farmer would ever sow broccoli seeds and expect to get potatoes? However, in the Church, we seem to expect to harvest outcomes that are contrary to the seed that we have sown. For example, we might be praying for more people to come to Christ, and yet we fail to deposit any seeds of God's love into those we are praying for.

> We seem to expect to harvest outcomes that are contrary to the seed that we have sown

Think about it: the moment we come to God and repent of sin, we receive His instantaneous forgiveness. However, His pardon does not negate the harvest we may still reap from our past actions. We are forgiven completely, yes, but there is often a journey of moving past the harvest of wrongs we have already committed. Seeds produce a harvest.

## SOWING PURPOSEFUL SEED

Farmers understand that sowing their best seed intentionally – in the right place and at the right time – carries the best promise for their future security.

- You can't harvest a great marriage without sowing honor to your spouse.
- You can't harvest victory with seeds of despondency.
- You can't harvest unity after sowing seeds of discord.
- You can't harvest lasting success with seeds of compromise.
- You can't harvest financial breakthrough without financial seeds.

Why? – because seeds produce after their own kind.

## SEEDS REQUIRE FERTILE ENVIRONMENTS

The Parable of the Sower, which Jesus told in *Matthew 13*, gives us many valuable lessons about sowing and harvesting. Perhaps most surprisingly, Jesus tells the disciples that the whole principle of sowing seed is a heavenly secret that is given to them and not others to understand. It is something you grasp by revelation, and if you don't receive the revelation, you won't experience the release.

> **If you don't receive the revelation, you won't experience the release**

*Matthew 13:10-11 The disciples came to him and asked, 'Why do you speak to the people in parables?' He replied, 'Because the knowledge of the secrets of the kingdom of heaven has been given to you, but not to them.' (NIV)*

We can accept the idea of harvest, yet fail to create the right environment for the harvest. In the natural world, seeds need fertile soil, moisture, food, warmth and sunlight. In the verses below, Jesus explains why only a proportion of seed planted actually bears good fruit.

*Matthew 13:18–23 Therefore hear the parable of the sower: When anyone hears the word of the kingdom, and does not understand it, then the wicked one comes and snatches away what was sown in his heart. This is he who received seed by the wayside. But he who received the seed on stony places, this is he who hears the word and immediately receives it with joy; yet he has no root in himself, but endures only for a while. For when tribulation or persecution arises because of the word, immediately he stumbles. Now he who received seed among the thorns is he who hears the word, and the cares of this world and the deceitfulness of riches choke the word, and he becomes unfruitful. But he who received seed on the good ground is he who hears the word and understands it, who indeed bears fruit and produces: some a hundredfold, some sixty, some thirty.*

**Some seed falls by the wayside** – This is when we respond to the principles of seedtime and harvest enthusiastically but carry no real revelation of their truth. The enemy comes and snatches it away, and we are left with no seed and, therefore, no harvest and no change.

**Some seed falls on stony places** – This is similar to the seed that fell by the wayside. It is when we respond with immediate joy, but we endure only for a while, and give up in the face of challenge and doubt.

**Some seed falls among thorns** – This is when we become seduced by the allure of material distractions. This doesn't happen overnight, but it works its deception over time. For many, this is a bigger issue than they realize.

Harvest requires the right seed in the right soil

**Some seed falls on good ground** – This is when we carry and activate the divine law of seedtime and harvest. We are committed, no matter what, to continue to sow. This will produce 100 times, 60 times, 30 times. I love how Jesus began at a hundred-fold. Harvest requires the right seed in the right soil.

## SEEDS ARE SUBJECT TO SEASONS

Some people say: 'I have sown, but I haven't seen an outcome yet.' The truth is, we don't see harvest in every season in the natural world. But no matter what happens, farmers continue to sow for harvest because they understand that, even if one year the produce is poor, seeds will still produce a harvest in the following year.

**Ecclesiastes 11:4** *Farmers who wait for perfect weather never plant. If they watch every cloud, they never harvest.* (NLT)

What we do know is that our seed determines what God is able to do on our behalf. Remember, God responds to our response.

**Psalm 126:5-6** *Those who sow in tears shall reap in joy. He who continually goes forth weeping, bearing seed for sowing, shall doubtless come again with rejoicing, bringing his sheaves with him.*

## UNPLANTED SEEDS FAIL TO PRODUCE

Here is an interesting thought: harvest requires seeds to come out of their packaging. It's interesting that we talk about good intentions a lot at funerals. The longer we live, the longer the list is of the things we wish we would have or could have done. This remains true whenever it comes to gaining new *Bible*-based revelation. We can meet it enthusiastically, but unless we are prepared to embrace it and plant it, neither we nor our world will experience change.

> Harvest requires seeds to come out of their packaging

In whatever area you need a harvest, stop making excuses and start planting seeds. Challenge procrastination, engage perseverance and plant the kind of seeds today that you desire to harvest tomorrow.

In the next chapter, we will take a look at the third foundational principle for managing our money wisely – saving to create a generational legacy.

# TWENTY-NINE

# 'SAVING' – INVESTING IN A GENERATIONAL LEGACY

---

I had an acquaintance who would proudly boast that he'd consider his life had been successful if 'on the day I die, I see my last check bounce or my last dollar spent'. He was (hopefully) joking, but this kind of attitude, even in the Church, is all too prevalent. I'm not sure whether this mind-set is based on a theology of 'Jesus is coming soon', a self-focused attitude, or a belief that the generations beyond our own are unimportant.

When it comes to leaving a legacy for the future, the enemy wants us to have no part of it. Yet the *Bible* presents the opposite view.

> **When it comes to leaving a legacy for the future, the enemy wants us to have no part of it**

***Proverbs 13:22*** *A good man leaves an inheritance to his children's children.*

Today, we are surrounded by a barrage of advertising that repeatedly shouts: 'You need it, and you need it now.' Our world of instant gratification has developed humorous monikers for the baby boomers who declare they are 'spending it all now and leaving nothing for the kids' – and it seems there are large numbers of them.

In the United States, they've coined a name for people with more than a million dollars in investments who want to consume their last penny about the same time as they take their last breath. They call them 'die brokers'. According to one *Forbes* magazine report, they have no plan to leave anything to charity. In the UK, 'gray beards' who spend up large on things like sports cars are said to be 'SKI-ing': 'Spending the Kids' Inheritance'. And in Australia, an insurance company found 80 percent of 'gray nomads' – the campervan crowd who tour the Outback – are living by the 'SKIN' principle: 'Spending the Kids' Inheritance Now'.

This approach couldn't be further from God's plan when it comes to money and material things. We are encouraged from scripture to live with a generational mind-set, so much so that we will leave a good inheritance – a legacy – not just for our children, but also for our children's children.

## Legacy's vision goes far beyond any individual

Legacy's vision goes far beyond any individual. We are called to build an inheritance that will continue to bless God's kingdom long after we are no longer on earth. To reprise A. W. Tozer's comments: 'Any temporal possession can be turned into everlasting wealth,' and, 'Whatever is given to Christ is immediately touched with immortality.'

## THE PRINCIPLE OF MULTIPLICATION

We've all probably heard the story of the 'widow's mite', but if the storyline of that encounter is elusive, let me remind you. In *Mark 12*, Jesus is sitting opposite the temple treasury and 'people watching' as townsfolk come by to make their contributions to the temple (storehouse). It is interesting that He sat and watched what people gave. Jesus understood the potential hold money has on people and the importance it carries.

*Mark 12:41-44 And many who were rich put in much. Then one poor widow came and threw in two mites, which make a quadrans. So He called His disciples to Himself and said to them, 'Assuredly, I say to you that this poor widow has put in more than all those who have given to the treasury; for they all put in out of their abundance, but she out of her poverty put in all that she had, her whole livelihood.'*

What she gave, the scholars tell us, was two very small copper coins worth a fraction of one US dollar. I took some time to look at what those mites would have become now if someone had invested them back in biblical times. Believe it or not, by the wonder of compounding interest, modern-day economists have estimated that if those two small coins (estimated at 80 US cents in today's money) had been deposited at the bank in the first century, bearing 4 percent compounding interest annually for 1,987 years, they would be worth an unbelievable **US$5,601,89 7,700,651,769,057,217,320,908,226,560 – or approximately $5.6 decillion.** And no, this is not a typo. Just 80 cents invested over many generations has the potential to change the world.

According to the Economist Intelligence Unit, at the time of writing *God Money & Me*, the current world public (government) debt is approximately **US$58,354,188,444,406 or $58 trillion**. Also, the October 2016 International Monetary Fund Fiscal Monitor Report declared that the total global debt of the non-financial sector was **US$152 trillion** – comprising the general government, households and non-financial firms. For the sake of this exercise, let's compare the total world debt of **$152 trillion** with what the widow's mites would be worth today if invested (**$5.6 decillion**). If invested long term, the mites would not only have wiped out current world debt, they would have been able to do it **36.8 quintillion (36,800,000,000,000,000,000) times over**! Simply mind blowing.

I have given you this illustration to demonstrate that we can change the future if we commit to SAVE. It's a dramatic reminder of the importance of investment and the power of multiplication at work. A little invested today can secure an ever-enlarging tomorrow. I understand the widow gave to God and was honored for doing so, and we have already covered the importance of stewarding and seeding. But my point here is that saving and investing will change the foundation of the generations that follow us.

We can so easily fall into the trap of believing we have nothing that could create a legacy. Unless we take something from what we have today and put it aside for tomorrow, this will be true. Remember, a little invested today can secure an ever-enlarging tomorrow.

---

**A little invested today can secure an ever-enlarging tomorrow**

---

This is precisely where everything began to change for me. As I have already outlined, the principle of good stewardship, that is, returning God's tithe to His house, was something I had grown up embracing. For a long time, I was also committed to the principle of seeding, even though I never understood it like I do today. However, I had never really considered this third ingredient when creating a financial pathway – the principle of saving for the next generation or investing to leave a legacy.

## HANDS OFF!

One more important point: I would describe this saving element as 'untouchable'. The whole idea is that this is an investment into the future of those who come after us – it is not to be consumed by us for our needs or wants. It is to be used only for what will increase our net worth and ultimately continue to live on beyond us.

Another key to remember in your saving is that this money should not be directed towards a holiday or anything that can depreciate in value. If you find yourself currently in debt, I would suggest that your savings should first go to reducing your debt. This will mean that from day one, you are already walking away from debt and toward financial freedom. I would encourage most people to have your saving percentage go into creating and building an asset in your personal home, which will provide a financial foundation to leave a legacy for your children's children. Our saving is what is designated to go generational.

Can you imagine how different your life would have been, and would be today, if your grandparents had embraced this principle as part of their financial pathway? Today, you would have become the recipient of their pre-planned wisdom. By the time it reached you, you wouldn't have needed to spend your life savings on a house, and you could have been already positioned to become an answer to the needs of others.

You might be thinking, 'I don't have any way I could save for the generations that will come after me.' Well, when we get to Chapter 31, we'll explore a pathway that shows how saving can work in with the other three elements we've been discussing.

But first, let's take a look at the fourth component of our finances and the aspect of money management we probably all enjoy the most – spending. Here, I'll provide you with some guidelines for managing your spending so it doesn't manage you.

# THIRTY

# 'SPENDING' – SETTING TODAY'S PARAMETERS

---

If I could take you back a few years, you might be very surprised to see how Maree and I lived and the choices we made around our spending. When we were first married, we didn't own anything apart from some very simple appliances, as we had given so much away. This resulted in us having to be incredibly careful with our budgeting. We would search the supermarket for the cheapest loaf of bread. We would buy luncheon sausage instead of ham and were always looking for the sale of the century (if you get what I mean).

As we had to finance most of our wedding ourselves, it took at least eight months to pay it off, even with the benefit of someone giving us low rental on our accommodation. We made the tough decision that we wouldn't purchase anything we couldn't pay for in cash. Looking back on it now, it

> We wouldn't purchase anything we couldn't pay for in cash

was one of the wisest decisions we made. The reality was, for the first six months, we didn't even have a washing machine. We couldn't afford to buy one, so we literally washed our clothes in the bath. We didn't even have the money to buy laundry detergent at times, so we would use cakes of soap because it was more economical. I remember walking up and down in the bath on top of the clothes trying to work up a lather, then rinsing them all many times over, twisting the water out and then hanging them up to dry.

After six months of being the human washing machine, I will never forget the joy of saving up enough to buy an old second-hand twin tub. If you are old enough to know what one of those is, you would know that today we wouldn't even call that a washing machine. It was completely manual and could only wash three or four shirts at a time but, for us, it was like heaven had opened.

We had to think carefully about the price of every meal and so many other things relating to money. Over those early years, we simply had no choice but to find a way, which sometimes meant we had people living with us, simply to help pay the rent.

Maybe today you feel like you could never change the way you live and spending patterns. The truth is, you probably never will, unless you commit to a season of 'delayed gratification' and downsizing your spending. If we could subordinate our spending to our commitment to create a pathway to financial freedom, we would change everything about our tomorrow.

## We must live within our means to make our future meaningful

Today, all too often, we place no restraint on what we think are the 'must haves'. If you find yourself struggling to create a financial future, you will need to make a decision about what you see as most important. Will you honor God by positioning Him sovereign over your financial world and by returning His tithe? Will you activate a harvest by the investment of seed into good soil? Will you link your investment into the future to mirror your seed with saving? For this to happen, we will have to limit our spending. We must live within our means to make our future meaningful.

## THE POWER OF DELAYED GRATIFICATION
Over the past 50 years, the 'Marshmallow Test' has become synonymous with temptation and willpower. As *The Atlantic* reports, Stanford Professor Walter Mischel's work on the Marshmallow Test 'permeates popular culture'. 'There are "Don't Eat the Marshmallow!" T-shirts, and Sesame Street episodes where Cookie Monster learns delayed gratification so he can join the Cookie Connoisseurs Club. Investment companies have used the Marshmallow Test to encourage retirement planning.'

As the lead researcher in studies that began in the 1960s and continued for 40 years, Mischel put a plate with one marshmallow on it in front of hundreds of four- and five-year-olds and offered them a deal. (He's explained recently they weren't the big puffy pink and white marshmallows we all imagine, but 'teeny, weeny pathetic miniature ones'.) The researcher, whom the kids knew and trusted because they'd played with him earlier, explained he was going to leave the room – and leave them with the marshmallow – for a little while. If the child did not eat the marshmallow while he was away, then they would be rewarded with, not only the initial marshmallow, but also a second marshmallow when he returned. However, if the child decided to eat the first one before the researcher came back, then they would not get a second marshmallow.

So the choice was simple: one treat right now or two treats later. The researcher then left the room for 15 minutes. The footage of what happened next is very entertaining: some kids jumped up and ate the marshmallow the minute he left the room. Others tried to avoid temptation and wriggled and bounced and moved their chairs, but most eventually gave in. Only a few children resisted the temptation and left the marshmallow intact.

## WHAT HAPPENED NEXT

The interesting part is what happened over the next 40 years. In follow-up tests, this group of children were studied in all areas of life, and the ones who had been able to delay their gratification and not eat the marshmallow outscored the rest on most measures of success – from higher academic achievement to less drug abuse, lower obesity, better response to stress, and better outcomes generally in a whole range of measures. Their parents reported them as generally more competent, even if they didn't know whether their children had eaten the marshmallow or not.

The researchers were forced to conclude that being able to delay gratification is a key strategy for success in many areas of life. In their words: 'Success usually comes down to choosing the pain of discipline over the ease of distraction.'

Even more interestingly, follow-up research showed self-control was a learned skill rather than a naturally acquired trait. If a child was promised a reward but never received it, they concluded very quickly that the researcher was not to be trusted and ate the marshmallow instantly. But if they found the researcher to be reliable, and delivered on promised rewards, they waited an average of four times longer. As one report noted: 'Just a few minutes of reliable or unreliable experiences were enough to push the actions of each child in one direction or another.'

> Success usually comes down to choosing the pain of discipline over the ease of distraction

Our spending is vitally important, yet should remain in the fourth place of priority.

## KEYS TO LIMITING YOUR SPENDING

### ONE – EMBRACE A DECISION TO LIVE WITHIN YOUR MEANS

The principle of delayed gratification is an absolute key. Wherever you are on this journey, and at whatever level you decide to begin limiting spending of your disposable income (which we'll look at further in Chapter 31), understand that, by doing this, you are under way to creating a financial future. Tomorrow's breakthrough lives within predetermined boundaries.

> Tomorrow's breakthrough lives within predetermined boundaries

In the majority of cases, we simply don't need to spend what we think we need to spend – or are led to believe we need to spend. If we fail to create a predetermined budget, we will mostly fail to make the changes we need to make.

### TWO – FIND A WAY TO INCREASE YOUR INCOME

Never underestimate your potential. It is sometimes as simple as turning the TV off, using what I call unproductive time (which we all have), and committing to prepare ourselves to become trained for a better job. If you seriously can't afford to live on what remains of your income after tithing and taxes, find a way to increase your income. For many seasons in my life, my only way forward was to work two jobs. Remember, where you find yourself today is not the end of the story. Preparation is the prerequisite to provision.

### THREE – SET UP ACCOUNTABILITY PARTNERS

The enemy continues behind the scenes to find ways to restrict you. He will do all he can to cause you to believe that this is beyond you. The truth is: once we break mammon off our money, honor God's way and live with wisdom, everything begins to change. For many of us, money is a topic we don't address, so it remains in the dark. Setting up financial accountability partners is crucial to combatting the enemy's plans to limit us in this area. I believe we need to have someone whom we trust, someone who has broken through in their financial world and who has our best interests at heart, to hold us accountable for our financial decisions. Accountability connects our decisions to the right outcome.

> **Accountability connects our decisions to the right outcome**

## FOUR – GOOD AND BAD DEBT – DON'T GO INTO DEBT FOR DEPRECIATING ASSETS

I mentioned briefly that if you find yourself in debt, your goal should be to reduce your debt first through your saving percentage. Here are a couple of other thoughts about debt.

I don't think it's necessarily wrong to borrow for an appreciating asset. What that means is something that grows in net value. The best example for most of us would be the purchase of a home. Having said that, I would never buy a home that required a level of debt that would inhibit my ability to control the future decisions that God wanted me to make.

A depreciating asset is anything that loses value. I remember passing through an airport where a new car was on display with some large advertising on the side. It said it could be bought for zero down payment and zero interest. At first glance, you would think, 'What an amazing deal.' But what it didn't say was, once you committed to buy it, it would drop in value by more than $10,000 the minute you drove it away. The key is this: don't spend what you don't have. When it comes to buying anything that will devalue, wisdom says: 'If you haven't got the cash, don't buy it.'

**Proverbs 22:7** *The rich rules over the poor, and the borrower is servant to the lender.*

So, if you ever find yourself having borrowed for anything that now restricts you from making the right decisions, you must change it. If your current mortgage is stopping you from embracing God's best plan for you, I would lower my positive debt to a level that enables me to get back in the driver's seat. This could even mean downsizing your home. We can never allow debt to become the loudest voice.

> We can never allow debt to become the loudest voice

It's not that God is against debt itself: God is against anything that is able to gain the position of lordship over us. I'm not saying you can't borrow; I'm saying just be careful. Everything that is a debt will have to be faced and repaid one day.

# THIRTY-ONE

# FROM PRINCIPLE TO PRACTICE – THE '10/10/10/80 PRINCIPLE'

This is where all the questions that we've explored – such as 'What do I tithe on?', 'How can I support other ministries?', 'How am I ever going to save?' and 'What if I can't afford to do it?' – come together and start to make sense. It's something I call the **'10/10/10/80 PRINCIPLE'**, and it's the pathway that brings together all the things no one ever told me about finances when I was younger.

If you are good with math, you will already be saying, 'But 10 + 10 + 10 + 80 equals more than 100! And what does that leave me to live on?' Yes, this might sound a little confusing, and we'll need to get our heads around things like how we account for tax (which we agreed back in Chapter 26 was an important part of the equation). But stick with me, and let's take a closer look together.

At the outset, let me give you a diagram that we can refer as we go. This illustrates how the four ways to use finances – stewarding, seeding, saving and spending – work together. It may be helpful to think of each element as a separate 'container' or 'account' into which we put our increase.

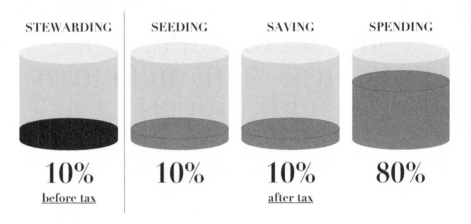

Maree and I had always tithed and given generously, but we had not understood the importance of seeding and saving alongside stewarding, while still allowing for spending. When we got a right perspective on how all four elements work together, everything changed. This is where the **'10/10/10/80 PRINCIPLE'** gets its name because, after allowing for the 10 percent tithe before tax, we divided our remaining disposable income into 10 percent for seeding, 10 percent for saving, and 80 percent for spending.

**Step 1** – The first 10 percent (in the left-hand container) is our tithe – it belongs to God and we are merely the stewards of it. As covered in Chapter 26, stewarding is the first element – we are to position Him first in our finances. Our tithe should be returned to Him before everything else, including tax obligations. After our tithe, we have to pay our tax, which belongs to the government. This is indicated by the line separating the first (stewarding) container from the rest of the diagram.

**Step 2** – After that, God says we have the responsibility to put a plan in place for what remains, which I call our 'disposable income'. In the diagram, this appears as the three containers on the right side of the line. The goal is to figure out how to best apportion this remaining amount across the other three elements: seeding, saving and spending. Things will be much easier if we have a plan in advance, so that each time we increase, we have already predetermined that all four containers will receive a percentage of that increase. Remember, if you manage your money, it won't manage you.

## Remember, if you manage your money, it won't manage you

It begins with seeding, and you'll see I'm recommending we put 10 percent of our disposable income into this container. As we saw in Chapters 27 and 28, seeds unlock a harvest of the same kind as the seeds that are sown. So, financial seeds unlock a financial harvest. The *Bible* speaks of the importance of seed, the principle of the harvest, and how He responds to us when we sow cheerfully and give generously. As we discussed, seeding is to be used beyond ourselves wherever we feel led by God to do it.

**Step 3** – The next step entails matching our saving to what we have put into our seeding container. As we discussed in Chapter 29, God's plan is for us to leave a legacy for the generations to come, and saving is our generational investment plan. If we can allocate 10 percent of our disposable income to saving (like we do for seeding), the principle of multiplication will see this grow and become an appreciating asset base, setting the foundation for financial freedom for the generations that follow us. As mentioned, our saving container is not meant to be consumed by us, it is how we establish an inheritance for our children's children. If we can't achieve this at once, it is something we should increase over time.

I seriously believe that if we don't match our saving to our seeding, we can end up like Maree and I ended up at 38 – married for 15 years with nothing – because we'd given so much away. I remember preaching a message entitled: 'God doesn't want you to give everything away'. It was possibly one of the most well-received messages I have ever preached (ha ha). Seriously though, the point I am making is that if we teach the farmer to bring all his seed to the offering, he will have no future harvest and his ability to bless others diminishes dramatically in the future.

## God doesn't want you to give everything away

**Step 4** – At this point, many of you might still be stuck on the thought that there is no way you could live on 80 percent of your current disposable income (after tithing and paying tax). The major challenge for most of us comes in the fourth ingredient, as it is to do with what we believe we need to live – our spending. You may be saying, 'But if I were to steward God's first tenth, pay tax, seed 10 percent of what is left, and save another matching 10 percent after that, then that would leave me just 80 percent of my disposable income to live on. And right now, I am struggling to believe I can exist on all of it.' Yet, hard or impossible as this may seem right now, I believe that getting these four elements right opens up a financial pathway both for us and those who follow.

What we initially see as God's price tag simply reads: 'Please trust me! If you honor Me with the first, I will bless the remainder and teach you how to live in a way of blessing, free from the control of mammon.'

Today, we have many people – including children and teens – who have already been doing this for years. Recently one young man aged 17 told me he already had $6,000 in his saving account (which he has invested into an appreciating asset). From his childhood, he has embraced the **'10/10/10/80 PRINCIPLE'**.

He is already light years ahead of many of his peers and maybe even some of us. He has honored God by stewarding, sowing seed, and saving for his tomorrow and that of others, while still being able to spend and live. If we all had dealt with our finances like this from a young age, imagine the difference in the financial future we would be experiencing today.

Simply put, God's way works. He always works generationally, and we too can change the cycles of lack when we live with a mind-set that looks beyond our own generation. Once we grasp this revelation and embrace these four ingredients, we will alter our future completely. We will no longer be trapped into living according to every wind of fortune or misfortune that blows our way. Instead, we'll have a firm foundation for creating a financial future.

## SO WHERE DO I START?

Living on 80 percent of your disposable income may not be realistic for you right now. But the key to anything of value is to commit to start somewhere: to set the wheels in motion. Don't give up or be disheartened. These principles are a goal that most of us can work towards, no matter how long it takes to get there.

> The '10/10/10/80 PRINCIPLE' is a goal that most of us can work towards

For many, I have encouraged them to begin with the first step – stewarding (returning to God His tithe or first tenth) – as I seriously don't believe, based on scripture, that we cannot return to God His full tithe. Then, make a start somewhere on the second and third steps of matching seeding to saving. Remember, as you sow some seed, you release a harvest.

If you really believe these suggested levels of seeding and saving are impossible for you right now, an alternative suggestion could be (after tithe and tax) to start with 2 percent seeding, 2 percent saving and 96 percent spending. Whatever the levels, the key is to always match what you seed to what you save. This would mean you would need to restrict your spending to 96 percent of your disposable income. Start somewhere and grow it every six months or annually as the Lord begins to bless you. For example, move from 10/2/2/96 (if it is really hard at the start), and then go to 10/5/5/90. Wherever you begin, the optimum goal with our left-over disposable income is to work towards arriving at: 10 percent seeding, 10 percent saving, and 80 percent spending.

On the other hand, some may feel that the suggested levels of seeding and saving are relatively easy to achieve as they already have a good asset base and ample income to live financially blessed. If you have done well financially, my question to you is, 'What if you took the **'10/10/10/80 PRINCIPLE'** further?'

Over the years, some people have said to me, 'I want to be able to double tithe.' My response has simply been, 'We can't double tithe. Tithing is the first 10 percent.' So why not consider spending just 50 percent of your disposable income and seeding 25 percent and saving 25 percent? You can increase your giving (seed), but if you do, I would encourage you to continue to match your percentage of saving (further investing) to your seed. For those entrepreneurs out there, you could then use your saving to invest in enlarging your financial capacity to create even greater opportunities for generosity.

Earlier on, I mentioned Robert Laidlaw, who was a great New Zealander and such an inspiration to many as a Christian businessman. He was a key force in one of the country's most successful and admired department stores, the Farmers Trading Company. For much of his life, Laidlaw donated half of his earnings to a range of largely evangelical causes and charities, dispensing grants through the Bethesda Charitable Trust. Later in his life, he reached the position he had dreamed about, where he could live on only 10 percent of his increase and give 90 percent of it away.

What an incredible life and example. However, if I was talking to him today, I would still encourage him to follow the template we've been developing – of matching your seeding to your saving – rather than giving 90 percent away. As we have seen, this enables us to invest in a greater long-term return, not only for our children's children, but also to increase our ability and capacity to release more through our investments. If you have been blessed financially, I encourage you – once you have set a good foundation of inheritance for your children's children – to continue to increase the percentage of your seeding and saving.

## ALL SUFFICIENCY AND AN ABUNDANCE FOR EVERY GOOD WORK

I want to once again draw your attention to the catalyst scripture that changed everything for me. I trust by the end of reading *God Money & Me*, you will know it off by heart.

*2 Corinthians 9:8 And God is able to make all grace abound toward you, that you, always having all sufficiency in all things, may have an abundance for every good work.*

God's word has undeniable authority. When we discover we are unable to figure it out or make things work on our own, that's a good time to trust God's word and to walk His way. According to *2 Corinthians 9:8*, it should be normal Christian living to have an abundance for every good work, far beyond simply existing. In just one generation of living the financial freedom principles I have described, we could set up the next generation to experience a lifetime of financial freedom.

You may still be saying: 'I can't ever see myself reaching those levels. I've been struggling to keep my head above water my whole life.' I am sure we can all offer a dozen reasons why we can't limit our spending and can't redirect some of our income to seeding and saving. The moment we begin to think it is OK for others but impossible for us, we are allowing our excuses to have the authority to decide our future. Without doubt, this will also be the way we are equipping our future generations. Don't give excuses the authority to decide your future. If this is you, you need to take some time and marinate yourself in the word of God and get a new revelation for yourself of God's plan for you to be 'blessed to be a blessing'.

> **Don't give excuses the authority to decide your future**

If I could encourage you in one thing, it's this: no matter where you begin, make it your goal to live financially in a way that honors God and sets up the generations to come. The truth is, as soon as you begin to see your stewarding, seeding, saving and spending containers start to function, you will begin to experience freedom in your financial world. When we know, first and foremost, that we have honored God with our finances, we are now in a position where we have begun our journey to financial freedom. Our today finds purpose once we attach tomorrow to it.

> **Our today finds purpose once we attach tomorrow to it**

## IMAGINE – IMAGINE – IMAGINE

As we bring *God Money & Me* to a close, may I encourage you that God fully loves and believes in you? He has so much more for you to experience and He simply asks all of us to trust Him as His way works.

Bethel Pastor Bill Johnson has said: 'The greatest vacuum on the planet is the knowledge of God's goodness.' I agree with him. We struggle to accept that God really is good, that He loves us and that He is a multiplier. It's hard for us to believe that God actually longs for us to flow into the freedom and the blessing of who He is in every area of our lives. Often we put our trust in other things, and settle for just trying to make it through.

Imagine if, through your obedience and trust in God, your grandchildren or the generations that follow you received an inheritance that enabled them to experience the lives God planned for them in *2 Corinthians 9*. Remember, that's where we are told:

*2 **Corinthians 9:8** And God is able to make all grace abound toward you, that you, always having all sufficiency in all things, may have an abundance for every good work.*

It may take as long as a generation to live out what we never grew up understanding about establishing a financial future. But it will totally be worth it. Live God's way with money and immediately, God has promised, we will see Him do the impossible.

*Malachi 3:10-12 'Bring all the tithes into the storehouse, that there may be food in My house, and try Me now in this,' says the Lord of hosts, 'If I will not open for you the windows of heaven and pour out for you such blessing that there will not be room enough to receive it. And I will rebuke the devourer for your sakes, so that he will not destroy the fruit of your ground, nor shall the vine fail to bear fruit for you in the field,' says the Lord of hosts; 'And all nations will call you blessed, for you will be a delightful land,' says the Lord of hosts.*

This book is simply about who God really is, who we are called to be and about what takes place when money enters the equation. It is about living a financial pathway that works and has God's blessing all over it – about each one of us becoming blessed to be a blessing.

**Proverbs 13:22** *A good man leaves an inheritance to his children's children.*

# MONEY'S PATHWAY

God provides every Christian with an invitation to live an abundant life. However, financial abundance involves the combination of four very important ingredients – stewarding, seeding, spending and saving. Becoming a good steward of the resources we receive begins with positioning God first. We then are to move from 'need' consciousness to a 'seed' consciousness. It is when we fully grasp God's principle of seedtime and harvest that everything begins to turn around.

But that is not the end. We then add saving and spending to the financial equation, and then a financial pathway begins to be prepared. It is when we live by bringing all four together that we break through the stronghold of lack. Not only do we unlock God's blessing in our material world, but we are empowered to create a generational legacy.

## MAIN REFLECTION POINTS:

1. Have you lived with a focus on the four areas of stewarding, seeding, saving and spending? If so, how? If not, which ones are the areas you need to make changes in?

2. Briefly describe your understanding of stewarding. Also, what is your greatest challenge when it comes to honoring God with His tithe?

3. Briefly describe your understanding of seeding. How do you see seeding as being different to stewarding?

4. Saving is what creates a generational platform of financial release. What, according to Chapter 29, is the main key to what we do in regards to seeding and saving?

5. Finish this quote: 'Remember, if you manage money, it won't _____ you.'

6. Spending requires we live within our means. Give your perspective of what 'delayed gratification' means to you right now.

7. What does the **'10/10/10/80 PRINCIPLE'** mean? How do we start creating a financial pathway if this is too big a step?

# ABOUT THE AUTHOR

---

Paul and his wife Maree are the pioneers and Senior Leaders of LIFE, a church comprising four main focuses: Church, Community, Business and Kingdom (www.lifenz.org). LIFE began in 1991 in Auckland, New Zealand, and today is a multi-campus, multinational church committed to see its city changed, its nation influenced and the world touched.

Under Paul and Maree's leadership, LIFE has continued to grow and today is home to multiple thousands of people. Through its Kingdom focus, many leaders and believers have been impacted through conferences held annually. LIFE also owns and is developing an increasing number of businesses, which fund an ever-expanding Community commitment.

Paul travels extensively, speaking at churches and leadership conferences globally. He also hosts LIFETV, a contemporary 'Meaningful answers to life' program, which now attracts a global audience (www.lifetv.co). Paul is also the inspiration for a leadership network and website www.pauldejongnz.com that continues to inspire and equip people from all streams of life. Paul's passion and mission is 'to live and lead by example' as he believes we only fully discover our potential when we live authentic, faith-inspired, God-dependent lives.

# PAUL & MAREE DE JONG
# RESOURCES

---

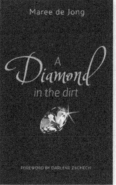

For more resources from Paul & Maree, check out:

## www.pauldejongnz.com

Follow Paul on:

## @pauldejongnz